£1-00

NEW ENGLISH DRAMATISTS 12

RADIO PLAYS

NEW
ENGLISH DRAMATISTS

12

RADIO PLAYS

Introduced by Irving Wardle

THE OBJECT
Giles Cooper

NO QUARTER
Barry Bermange

THE ANTS
Caryl Churchill

THE WHELKS AND THE CHROMIUM
Jeremy Sandford

THE LONG-DISTANCE PIANO-PLAYER
Alan Sharp

HAPPY DAYS ARE HERE AGAIN
Cecil P. Taylor

PENGUIN BOOKS

Penguin Books Ltd, Harmondsworth, Middlesex, England
Penguin Books Inc., 7110 Ambassador Court, Baltimore, Maryland 21207, U.S.A.
Penguin Books Australia Ltd, Ringwood, Victoria, Australia

—

All these plays first published in Penguin Books 1968
Introduction
Copyright © Irving Wardle, 1968
The Object
Copyright © Estate of Giles Cooper, 1968
No Quarter
Copyright © Barry Bermange, 1968
The Ants
Copyright © Caryl Churchill, 1968
The Whelks and the Chromium
Copyright © Jeremy Sandford, 1968
The Long-distance Piano-player
Copyright © Alan Sharp, 1968
Happy Days are Here Again
Copyright © Cecil P. Taylor, 1968

—

Made and printed in Great Britain
by Cox & Wyman Ltd,
London, Fakenham and Reading
Set in Monotype Bembo

CONTENTS

INTRODUCTION

AT a time when more playwrights than ever before are getting into print, the appearance of such a collection as this is long overdue. And if ever a group of writers deserved representation in a series devoted to new drama it is the radio dramatists of the past fifteen years. The group includes most of the big names in the British theatrical revival, some of whom might never have emerged without their early outlet in radio; and what must be stressed immediately is that the material they produced cannot be discounted as juvenilia. What they wrote for radio was often their best work. No one familiar with Giles Cooper only from the *Maigret* adaptations and a handful of not entirely satisfactory stage plays, could deduce his mastery as a radio dramatist. And John Mortimer, despite his career in the West End, has never produced anything better than his first play *The Dock Brief*, written for radio.

Without the persistence of the radio producer Nesta Pain, who was determined to extract a play from him, *The Dock Brief* would probably not have been written and Mortimer might well have remained a novelist. Radio is full of stories like this. The best known is probably that of *Under Milk Wood*, which was dragged out of Dylan Thomas page by page by the producer Douglas Cleverdon. Mortimer and Thomas, of course, were already established writers at the time. But the same kind of attention is also paid to novices to the B.B.C. who strike the Drama Department as promising. As such a novice myself who has so far failed to turn in anything worth performance I know at first hand the care and time the Department are prepared to expend without any certainty of repayment. Still, a good many writers have given handsome returns on the investment – Robert Bolt, Alun Owen, Ray Jenkins, Colin Finbow; and two of the discoveries of the sixties represented in this book, Caryl Churchill and Barry Bermange.

The B.B.C.'s Drama Department is the most comprehensive play-production organization in the country. It puts out something between 800 to 1,000 scripts a year (excluding *The Dales* and *The Archers*) and its service ranges across the whole dramatic spectrum, taking in middlebrow matinées for the captive wife, adaptations of stage successes and novels, the world classic repertoire, and original material. Here we are concerned only with the last category. It does not command the biggest audience, but it holds a key position on the British dramatic map. It has a double importance, both as the likeliest training ground for the aspirant writer and as an experimental sector where radio ceases to be a secondary medium and finds its own voice. And as the writer and the medium each have much to gain from the other, their relationship is reciprocal.

For new playwrights the all-important factor is that radio provides the only open door into the profession. Nothing can teach inexperienced writers more than seeing their work exposed in performance; and nowadays this experience is extremely hard to come by. In the early pre-war days of London's theatre clubs a writer like Frank Marcus could mount his apprentice plays for about £50 a week. Now even this modest platform has been removed; and apart from such stray events as the Royal Court's Sunday-night performances and the productions of the International Theatre Club, it is hard for the beginner to get any kind of professional foothold. Too many people and too much money are involved. Television, with its mass audience to feed, has steadily lost interest in the 'one-shot play' (to use its own hideous terminology). And a one-set West End show now devours over £6,000 in production costs plus weekly running costs of about £2,600. These are not areas where writers can make their mistakes and try again.

Radio, because of its cheapness, does provide such an area, and its economic advantages are underwritten by the structure and policy of the Drama Department. Under a Head of Drama (Martin Esslin) the Department consists of twenty-five producers and a script unit containing eight members and a script editor. The unit acts as a sorting house for whatever comes in and all the reading (except foreign language material) is done internally. It receives something between 100 and 200 unsolicited manuscripts a week, but according to Esslin all except the obviously utterly hopeless among them get read. This system is in sharp contrast with that of British television where each drama spot is controlled by a separate producer, interested only in what will fit his own series and where there is no central agency for handling unsolicited material. In radio there is never any danger of scripts drifting from one department to another in search of the right man. When material is rejected it is on grounds of quality, not because the writer has ignored series requirements or misaddressed the envelope.

The vast bulk of material, of course, is rejected. Of the yearly average of 7,500 manuscripts, only 300 at the most can be put into production. Still, considering the actual scarcity of writing talent, 300 is a large number; and the Department takes good care of the authors it does accept. In the case of a newcomer, the first move is to allocate his work to the appropriate programme; and to decide on the producer most likely to be sympathetic towards it. This marriage bureau approach often leads to lasting collaborations (as in the partnerships between Giles Cooper and Donald McWhinnie, and Colin Finbow and Charles Lefeaux). The producer starts as an adviser, giving the writer any help he needs with radio technique and dramatic construction; later, knowing better than anyone else how his colleague's mind works, he acts as a sensitive interpreter who is prepared to learn from his ex-pupil. As McWhinnie says in *The Art of Radio*, 'The writer's business is to make excessive demands of his interpreters.'

Once the partners are joined, the Department still presides over them as a fairy godmother, organizing conferences for writers and composers, and seminars on radio technique (a recent development which is now being established on a fairly regular basis). Also, knowing that writers are inclined to approach radio as a springboard into the higher-paying media, the Department have acquired the power to reward their own playwrights with a television option. As for money – one of the great deterrents to potential radio authors – the average fee for a commissioned ninety-minute script (the radio equivalent of a three-act stage play) is £200, less than half the television rate. However, with repeats and transcriptions the author can increase it to £750; and if, as sometimes happens, the work is sold to Germany (where the radio play as a genre has attracted far more interest than it has here), he can multiply the figure to about £2,000. So the reward for writing what you want for radio is not necessarily smaller than writing what the series producer wants for television.

The other great deterrent – radio's lowly position in the fashion market – is more serious. As McWhinnie puts it, radio was a millionaire before it was thirty. During the war and until the arrival of television it was the nearest thing we had to a national theatre; no actors were better known than Cecil Trouncer and Carleton Hobbs, and the products of the Rothwell House *avant-garde* were treated as major cultural events. It was an artificial situation, and not many of the verse dramas and poetic childhood evocations of the period would stand re-examination. But now the pendulum has swung to the opposite extreme. Radio, despite its continued role as the source of tomorrow's dramatists, remains the critic's Red China; large, potent, simmering with expansionist ambitions, and ignored. And for any writer, except star practitioners like Beckett and Pinter whose work is sure of attention in whatever form they select, this is deeply discouraging. Audiences for Saturday Night Theatre still may top 750,000; a production on the Third may net 100,000. But what good does it do? The author's only contact with them will be a handful of abusive letters. And he will be extremely lucky if he gets a three-line mention in any national newspaper.

The indifference of newspapers to radio productions is a subject in itself. It amounts to a kind of blindness. Writers whose work would be noticed if it were appearing for one night in a 500-seat theatre or in an edition of 3,000 copies, become invisible as soon as they produce anything for radio. I can't explain this. As a newspaper critic it seems self-evident to me that a new play by, say, Bernard Kops or Tom Stoppard ought to be reviewed for its own sake irrespective of the medium for which it happens to have been written. But arts page editors, even those with plenty of space to fill, are inclined to treat the medium as more important than the artist; they will find room for amateur stage productions of Kops's *Stray Cats and Empty Bottles* and Stoppard's *Rosencrantz and Guildenstern Are Dead*, but not for radio productions of the same authors' *Home Sweet Honeycomb* and *If You're Glad I'll Be Frank*. You might say that the best work gets lost under the dead weight of routine material, but if so you would expect the best television work to be buried in the same way. Whereas when television does originate something of quality, productions like Clive Exton's plays or Jeremy Sandford's *Cathy Come Home* which halt the random flux of entertainment and lodge themselves in the memory, their value is generally recognized at the time. Television, which can at least convert a miscellaneous domestic group into an audience, has some power to create an event. Radio, since the transistor took the place of the family wireless set, has no such power. It cannot impose itself on the attention. The listener has to create the event for himself, and this is too much like work for most of us. P. H. Newby, the Head of the Third Programme, once listed convenience as a main asset of modern radio; it seems to me to be radio's most crippling liability.

However necessary money is to the writer, what matters more is the chance to build a reputation; and where some playwrights can make as big a name in television as they could in the theatre, nobody makes a reputation from radio. The classic example is that of Bill Naughton, most of whose film and stage work had appeared first on radio without raising any kind of a stir. Thanks to his rare faculty for remaining creatively alive to the subject matter of a completed work, he has been able to rewrite for different media without getting stale; but although *Alfie* has been successfully reproduced as a stage play, a film, and a novel, Naughton has never improved on the original radio monologue. Needless to say, it has not been published.

The young writer who breaks into radio, then, endures the frustration of being discovered by the B.B.C. only to be ignored by the outside world. But obscurity does have a few advantages – one of them being freedom of speech. He can treat any subject he wants in any style he wants without considering the ratings or the box-office take; and without inflaming M.R.A. or the League of Midland Madwomen. One of the few cheering remarks ever attributed to Mrs Mary Whitehouse was her refusal to escalate the Clean-Up TV Campaign into a war on pornographic books. 'Why don't you do it?' she said; 'I'm too busy.' For as long as there are no fortunes to be made out of radio and no mass audience for it to be accused of corrupting, the radio playwright can escape the self-censorship of television and the theatre, and work with colleagues whose only interest is to do justice to his talent.

The laws of radio-writing differ from those of the theatre, but they provide the best initial training for any type of dramatic composition. As a one-dimensional medium radio saves the beginner from trying to learn half a dozen techniques at once and forces him to concentrate on the one element that matters most: language. Esslin lists the hallmarks of the tyro as: 'repetitiveness; too great a length of speeches; inability to realize that the audience doesn't know what the writer knows: miscalculation of how long a scene can be held.' This is pretty basic stuff, but there are plenty of stage practitioners who have never learnt it and manage to get away with flabby writing under the cover of visual business. And besides the basic equipment, radio dialogue is obliged to compensate for the missing visual dimension and the lack of physically present spectators. I don't believe there is any such thing as a 'captive audience'; if a stage playwright bores his public in the first fifteen minutes he has 'lost' them just as effectively as if they had switched him off at home. All the same, people who see stage productions go to the theatre with that intention; a large proportion of the radio audience come in by accident, and the writer's job is instantly to persuade them that it is worth staying on.

In basic terms, this means that the radio dramatist must at the outset find some way of hooking the listener's attention. He is in the position of a fairground barker trying to get through the crowd's defences. The difference, of course, is that he can't cheat; and whether he starts with a dark hint or a dead body, his opening must set up an accurate programme for what is to follow. Translated into more elevated terms, this approach to the audience represents one of the crucial distinctions between radio and the theatre. In *The Summing Up* Somerset Maugham defined theatrical talent as a mysterious knack, unconnected with the intellect, which consists simply of being able to put words together so that they hit the back wall of the house. Maugham was talking about the commercial theatre, but I think he expressed a general truth; and writers who do possess this gift for projection often have difficulty in modulating it when they get off-stage. Witness Shaw's letters; or John Osborne's telegrams. With radio the focus changes from the wrong end of a telescope to that of a microscope, and big gestures are replaced by nuances. However, this does not mean that projection becomes superfluous on radio, but that it needs projection of another kind; a voice pitched not to reach the back of the gallery, but the back of the listener's mind. Radio's auditorium is the human skull.

I first became aware of this not through any radio production but during a performance of Beckett's *How It Is* at the Traverse Theatre in Edinburgh. Half-way through this frantic monologue of a man drowning in mud the lights went off and the voice gabbled on in the dark. And with this blackout the action leapt from the physical acting area into the centre of the imagination, immediately gaining a visual clarity and emotional terror that were quite lacking before. It was more as though the lights had been turned on. This is radio's natural element; but it took a theatrical event to drive it home. Perhaps radio dramatists would get more recognition if instead of broadcast productions there were a few theatre clubs putting on shows in the dark.

Clearly these conditions are favourable only to certain types of drama. Elaborate ensemble plays, for instance, generally fail to work because if characters are not regularly heard they disappear. Radio, therefore, is ill-equipped to present Britain's favourite playwrights, Shakespeare and Chekhov (not to mention Shaw). There are exceptions, such as the magnificent Scofield-Ashcroft *Macbeth* – but as the essential action in that play takes place inside the hero's mind it might almost have been written for radio. With the more open plays, like the histories, the medium acts as an arbitrary filter, projecting the soliloquies at full strength and blurring the passages of ceremonial rhetoric and multiple relationships. There are other things that radio cannot do. It cannot handle a static experience (even Beckett acknowledges this principle). It cannot show a character in motion, except towards or away from the microphone (the one mistake Frank Marcus made in *The Killing of Sister George* was to show the radio heroine delivering her lines while riding a moped). As it has no equivalent for the permanent set it cannot show the relationship between developing character and fixed environment.

Such limitations have been recognized from the start, but it has taken writers a long time to convert them from a handicap into a source of strength. In the early days the most familiar figure in radio drama was the narrator whose job was to translate the performance into theatrical terms by spoon-feeding the audience with background detail and visual information. Narration is a legitimate radio device, but only when the speaker has the direct function of a story-teller (as in *Under Milk Wood*); when he is used merely to dodge the conditions of the medium he comes over as a superfluous middleman in a dinner-jacket. Pre-war writers also fell into the trap of assuming that because radio had nothing to give the eye it must give the ear a feast. Hence the extravagant vocal callisthenics in Tyrone Guthrie's experimental pieces, and the poetic documentaries of D. G. Bridson in which a trip round a steel factory would be hammed up with metaphors about 'rivers of boiling light that ache upon the eye'. Although even at the time there was an evident disparity between style and content, the same approach persisted through the war years when the shaky radio aesthetic was fortified by an alliance with the New Apocalypse poets, some of whom found a secure berth with the B.B.C. as members of an official *avant-garde*, and whose trusted formula of Christian imagery, classical fable, and Eliot-haunted diction gave rise to a long line of inert verse dramas.

Meanwhile, of course, the theatre was pursuing a similar mirage; a multi-level play combining the commercial appeal of *Private Lives* with the poetic significance of *The Waste Land*. And when this movement petered out with Christopher Fry, the theatre was left wandering in the desert until the rough beasts of 1956 slouched into Sloane Square to be born. On radio the revival had come some years earlier, though it was hardly noticed at the time. The irony is that radio found its own voice at the precise moment that it lost the mass public to television.

As the revival was part of a general change in the climate of taste it would be unrealistic to credit it to any one man. Still, one cannot pass over the contribution made by Donald McWhinnie in his years as Assistant Head of Drama. McWhinnie, whose published statements suggest a fastidious distaste for mass entertainment, devoted his main energy in radio to clearing a space for material he believed in, no matter how small its audience was likely to be. Both as a director and as a propagandist his only aim was to serve the author. Among other things he introduced British audiences to the plays of Anouilh, Ugo Betti, and Montherlant before anyone had chanced them in the theatre (under Esslin this process has continued with the first British productions of Max Frisch, Slawomir Mrozek, and Vaclav Havel). He also commissioned work from Beckett; and with as little encouragement from the Corporation's programme planners as from the outside world, he proceeded to develop the style of production which is radio's distinctive contribution to modern drama.

Radio happens in the mind. It is the art of the unspoken: the best means yet evolved for expressing 'lives of quiet desperation' which Thoreau ascribed to the mass of mankind. In its simplest form it is a commuter remorsefully surveying his wasted years while on his way to the office; or a middle-aged couple stretched out silently in the dark each wishing the other would die. If it had been invented 200 years ago it would still have had the same access to this area of experience. What came to McWhinnie's aid in the early 1950s was the fact that radio's natural range corresponded to one of the main upheavals in modern European literature: the emergence of individual consciousness as the only certain reality. Strindberg, in pieces like the *Dream Play* and the late chamber plays, had brought this mode of perception into the theatre by the turn of the century, but it was not until after the last war that European drama really caught up with the work of Joyce and Kafka. The result, when it did start moving, was the body of work known as the theatre of the absurd. Its characteristics are: the substitution of an inner landscape for the outer world; the lack of any clear division between fantasy and fact; a free attitude towards time, which can expand or contract according to subjective requirements; a fluid environment which projects mental conditions in the form of visual metaphors; and an iron precision of language and construction as the writer's only defence against the chaos of living experience. With the exception of the visual metaphors (and even those can often be translated into sound) that list defines the central territory of modern radio drama. The best known absurdist plays are works for the theatre; but what plays make more natural radio material than Ionesco's *Victims of Duty*, where the action extends from the sky to the ocean bed, or Beckett's *Endgame* which takes place inside a magnified skull? The dramatic idiom that has taken shape in the past fifteen years has considerably narrowed the gap between radio and the theatre.

Having made the point as dogmatically as that, I should stress once again that radio is one of the freest of media and much of its best work lies outside the absurdist idiom. Besides employing professionals it provides an outlet for all kinds of part-timers – senior Civil Servants, housewives, bus-drivers – who are the dramatic equivalent of Sunday painters, and share with them the capacity for producing talented work that owes nothing to prevailing fashion. Among the professionals, too, there is a wide variety of style, often so personal as to defy the dramatic categories. One of the most satisfactory forms, for instance, is the loose dramatic essay interweaving conversational narrative and dramatized episodes (John Mortimer is a master in this genre). Then there is the extravert storytelling of such writers as Simon Raven and Ian Rodger who deal with the real world and use radio's visual strength to evoke battlefields and Oxbridge glamour. There is straightforward comic fantasy, and straight internal monologue.

None of these is included here, but this collection does convey some of the variety as well as the quality of radio writing. The absurdists are represented in strength (Cooper, Bermange, Taylor). *The Ants* is a beautiful example of radio's gift for expanded metaphor – a territory of its own midway between poetry and the theatre. Jeremy Sandford's pleasure beach panorama shows the microphone challenging the film in visual reportage; and Alan Sharp demonstrates the combination of high-style narrative with music and colloquial dialogue.

Some of these writers are well known, and others will be familiar only to the radio public. The only safe comparison one can make between them is that the first group is more likely to contain those who are wholly dependent on writing for a living. For them, the conditions of the profession do not permit a total commitment to the small rewards and obscurity of radio. To some extent this is a healthy situation: writers, like actors, need to try everything before settling down. But it is also true that some natural radio writers have wasted too much creative energy, as Cooper did, adapting themselves to media in which they will never be at home.

Plays always require more work from the reader than novels, and radio plays, which depend even in performance on the audience's imaginative contribution, are particularly demanding in this respect. The process is akin to reading a musical score, and the reader may find it helpful to observe these tips. Never let the eye jump to the end of a sentence, but allow the words to have the impact they would possess in performance. Try to hear characters in terms of contrasted tone quality and rhythm (*The Object*, for instance, might be scored for tuba, viola, and oboe). Assume that the words on the page are only the tip of the iceberg (these authors rarely go in for 'literary' style or explicit statements of meaning); if the play is not working for you, it is more likely that your imagination is at fault than the playwright's.

Happy Days are Here Again, a piece originally written for the stage, is a good example of the interchangeability of absurdist theatre and absurdist radio – though it is not particularly representative of its author. Cecil P. Taylor is a Glasgow-Jewish playwright now in his late thirties whose work has been likened to a bannock bun topped off with sour cream and a chocolate hammer and sickle. To unscramble that indigestible image, Taylor's best known pieces, *Allergy* and *Bread and Butter*, have been set in and around Glasgow and show an intricate tug-of-war between Communist idealism, Jewish community loyalties, and non-ideological attachments. He can write excellent high-pressure comedy; but perhaps his main gift is his feeling for common humanity and for making the long littleness of life something worth looking at. The atmosphere comes through in this programme note: 'I walk through the park, watch my son swing on my old swing and fish in my old pond and relax on the green, rolling meadows. . . . Sometimes, it's enough. . . . Sometimes, it isn't.'

These plays, and his subsequent musical *Who's Pinkus? Where's Chelm?* were presented in London by the Traverse Company which also gave *Happy Days* its first showing in Edinburgh in 1965. This is a rather more derivative piece in the 'comedy of menace' style, though with a good deal more invention and sense of purpose than such exercises usually possess. And in the course of this macabre get-together by the ex-clients of an allegedly dying whore, Taylor manages to work in his characteristic themes. Liphitz, the avuncular pimp, is a monstrous caricature of the Jewish father, treating the clients as if they were unworthy marriage suitors, and playing on their guilt to extract handouts. He is a mixture of sadistic ringmaster, Eastern potentate, and silly old man; and he certainly makes the others dance. They include an abject capitalist, a superannuated rake, a pair of liberal hangers-on, and the proletarian engineer who finally accepts the whole burden of guilt and becomes the group's scapegoat. I'm not sure what comment is intended here on the class struggle, but I suspect that when Taylor wrote the play his Marxist mainspring was still intact. In the Edinburgh production the action was clogged by such episodes as the dragging in of Waxman's corpse and Liphitz's repeated coat and boots routine. Readers with a radio imagination will appreciate the power of non-visual performance to eliminate these distractions and establish the play more securely on the frontier between fact and fantasy.

The undisputed master of this territory was the late Giles Cooper, in my opinion the finest radio dramatist this country has produced. Cooper was a miniaturist; but just as a Fabergé jewel can contain as much workmanship as a fresco, so his plays pack in as much content as any comparable theatrical work (radio, in any case, moves faster than the theatre). Form and content are so inseparable in his writing that any attempt to split them up for analysis is liable to become an artificial game. Still, if one reads through several Cooper plays (a collection of six was published in 1966 by the B.B.C.) a clear view of his world does take shape. What comes through is a profound mistrust for the reassurances of civilized life, and an awareness of how little it takes to reduce man to an aggressive or terrified animal. Cooper is not really a psychological dramatist, and still less a social ideologist. Like Pinter (particularly in *The Homecoming*) he is concerned not with Freudian or economic man, but with the archetype of Robert Ardrey's *African Genesis*, territorial man: a creature less attached to his mate or his tribe than to his own bit of ground. This is not a heroic figure and Cooper does not deal in heroes. His characters are generally defeated by their environment, but there is no suggestion that such creatures deserve to win.

Nothing as explicit as this is to be found in Cooper's own dialogue which is allusive, witty, and rigorously economical. Once you've heard it, it seems the only possible way of writing for radio. Indeed, even before any such idiom was in use, the need for it was recognized. Louis MacNeice, though his own plays remained consciously literary productions, forecast the lines on which radio dialogue could profitably develop in the introduction to *Christopher Columbus*:

With a literature as old as ours and a contemporary diction so vulgarized, precise and emotive writing comes to depend more and more upon twists – twists of the obvious statement or the hackneyed image . . . . In radio, without sacrificing simplicity or lucidity, you can often leave the twisting to the voice.

On the page Cooper has to be read with care, as so many of his effects depend on the power of performance (where the eye can never race ahead) to emphasize the slight, but crucial, displacements of commonplace phrases. But even without the help of actors his technique can give pleasure in itself – like that of an athlete or a concert pianist, conveying a sensuous mastery of the instrument.

His plays fall into two main categories: those exploring the private fantasies of a character in a 'real' situation (such as his bathroom fantasia *Under the Loofah Tree*); and those which use a naturalistic opening as a springboard into a fantastic development (such as the nightmarish *Unman, Wittering and Zigo* and his masterpiece *Mathry Beacon*). *The Object*, which won the Czech International Radio Drama Prize in 1966, belongs to the second category. Of its three characters two are undisguised scavengers, and it is typical of Cooper that they should represent opposite extremes of intelligence and class. Gary may be a thick-witted prole incapable even of making a phone call, and Thurle an old-maidish schoolteacher given to tampering with little girls, but when a space capsule lands in the back garden they both rush for it like a pair of greedy dung beetles. There is no essential difference between Thurle's plan for selling it to Russia and Gary's idea of breaking it up to flog for a few bob in the market. Such is man's grafting nature: all Cooper will allow for them is that life is not on their side, and that the authorities are up to the same game.

According to McWhinnie, 'the sure test of a radio writer is the intensity with which he feels his text as a sound of voices'. And in a play like *The Object* it is this organization of material into a vocal pattern which makes one take it seriously as a comment on human behaviour. Drama is always a formal art; but with writers such as Cooper and Pinter, construction takes on the higher discipline of music. It is not simply a question of exploiting material thriftily and presenting a clearly developing action, but of converting the subject matter into thematic material and elaborating it in terms of counterpoint, modulation, timbre, and dynamics. The governing factor is not naturalistic probability but abstract composition. So if, in one sense, 'anything can happen' in a radio play, this freedom is counterbalanced by an added severity of the form. And I feel that the conclusion of *The Object* (unusually optimistic for this author) lacks conviction for formal reasons. As a stage dramatist Cooper always had trouble with his endings, and here there is no thematic preparation for the last-minute introduction of sexual fertility as the means by which Gary can change from an insect into a man. For once it seems that Cooper left a cliché untwisted.

The Ants, first broadcast in 1962 when the author was in her early twenties, again reduces human affairs to the level of insect life. It is the shortest and I think the most perfect play in this collection. Its strength as a radio piece is that it immediately hits the imagination with a bold metaphor from which the remainder of the action develops. In the foreground are the small boy and the old man observing the life of the ant-hill; in the background are the boy's estranged parents, squabbling their way towards divorce with no more human feeling than a pair of insects, and due for symbolic destruction at the end. The traditional alliance between youth and age provides a double perspective on the scurrying life in between; and the bleak conclusion on human withdrawal is so forcefully projected by the image that Caryl Churchill had no need to put it into words. Her clarity of purpose and technical precision make further discussion unnecessary.

The Whelks and the Chromium, another piece of convertible dramatic currency, has appeared on the stage as part of Jeremy Sandford's *Dreaming Bandsmen*. In its radio form it went out in 1958, which makes it the earliest piece in this book. And it is less a play than a documentary writer's day off; a profile of the Southend pleasure crowds by a man who loves them and knows how they speak. The tenuous romantic thread is only a pretext for evoking the whole scene; the girlie shows, the scenic railway, and the juke boxes; tactics for picking up and chatting up; tactics for brushing off and acting hard to get. The atmosphere is at once tawdry and glamorous. You might compare it with *Bartholomew Fair*. On radio they must have had great fun with the sound effects, but it is also great fun to read.

Alan Sharp made his name as the author of *A Green Tree In Gedde*, a best-selling novel of 1965 which followed a party of randy young Northerners on a pilgrimage from incest in Greenock to lesbian sadism in Germany. He writes a big pounding style which made an earlier appearance in 1962 in *The Long-distance Piano-player*, the only play here that features a narrator. Sharp's narrative is in the highly coloured, bardic vein popularized by Dylan Thomas, and on the page it isn't altogether sympathetic unless one has the aural imagination to hear it against the musical continuum. Essentially the play is a duet for narrator and piano. Other characters, even the marathon pianist himself, are subsidiary; and their spiritless colloquial exchanges are set in deliberate contrast with the elevated diction of the narrative. The primary dramatic appeal is that of an endurance test, as the player's increasing exhaustion is reflected in the music. As a parable it draws the romantic distinction between art and ordinary life, presenting the pianist's solitary ordeal as the price of rising above melancholy and boredom.

First broadcast in 1962, well before *Black Comedy* arrived on the stage, *No Quarter* again shows radio forecasting theatrical fashion; set in a decaying hotel in pitch darkness, the play exploits the Chinese reversal of lighting values which Peter Shaffer is customarily credited with having adapted for British use.

In other respects, *No Quarter* is very much a play of its time. Its atmosphere is one of mounting terror; its language that of common speech rearranged to produce effects of comic incongruity and veiled threat; its themes human solitude and the experience of waiting. However, the play is more than a whispering gallery for Beckett and Pinter. Barry Bermange may sometimes echo their cadences and proceed by the standard radio route from the familiar to the fantastic; but he soon passes into territory of his own. His dialogue has a hallucinatory power to dwell on commonplace objects until they become strange and hostile; showing environments which we take for granted and hardly even see, assuming a life of their own and recoiling against the human invader. And this mutation could hardly find a more alarming setting than a hotel, where visitors automatically expecting smoothly serviced anonymity discover the building rebelling under their feet, finally stranding them in vertiginous isolation under the night sky. The climax approaches the sensationalism of Victorian Gothick, but Bermange earns all his effects by thorough preparation.

IRVING WARDLE

GILES COOPER

The Object

The Object was first broadcast on the B.B.C. Third Programme on 17 April 1964 with the following cast:

GARY	Bernard Bresslaw
MILL	Sheila Grant
THURLE	Michael Hordern
TELEPHONIST	Molly Rankin
VOICE	Garard Green

Produced by Charles Lefeaux

Fade in a train pushing up an incline with some effort. It fades into the distance and there is a moment's silence followed by the near squeaking and twanging of an old bed.

GARY: That tin of beans, you know, that tin.

MILL: He come where I was, he said things.

GARY: Tin of baked beans. What things?

MILL: Things he said. I don't care. . . . I told him.

GARY: But that tin what we had last night, you know.

MILL: What tin? You wouldn't think they'd have the nerve. Well?

GARY: Is it thrown out?

MILL: No, there's beans in it. Well would you think? Because he's him; because I'm me. Do you want them beans?

GARY: I want the tin.

MILL: What for?

GARY: All tins. Down Blackway Common there's a fellow got a machine now, crushes tins, crush anything, cars and all. Gives a bob a hundred, tins . . . scrap.

MILL: Shilling a hundred's not much.

GARY: Still, something.

MILL: Oh something, something yes, but would you think? Like that.

GARY: Who was he then?

MILL: Some bloke; at work this was.

GARY: You want to tell them.

MILL: I did. Get as good money anywhere I said.

GARY: What did they say?

MILL: Said all right.

GARY: How was that? All right?

MILL: They gave me my cards.

GARY: No!

MILL: I can get something, easy.

GARY: I thought you liked it there.

MILL: I don't like being told.

GARY: All the same . . . what other tins we got?

MILL: There's some in the ditch.

GARY: What ditch?

MILL: Bottom of the garden where the bank comes down.

GARY: They're no good rusty. Ted was saying he wouldn't take them rusty.

MILL: Well, I don't know then.

GARY: You don't know, don't know. I know. Getting yourself sacked.

MILL: I've got my pride.

GARY: I've got my van. What about the van? What about the instalments: and the telly?

MILL: We don't get a picture.

GARY: Do you think you're helping to get one, do you?

MILL: But we don't.

GARY: Because we're behind.

MILL: The picture goes off when we're behind?

GARY: No! But they've forgot us, that firm's no good, they forget. If we go along and say we got no picture, ask for someone to come and mend it, they'll remember, then they'll want the money or they'll come and take it away.

MILL: Still . . .

GARY: Well you can listen; you said you liked to listen.

MILL: It's not the same though, only if you're in here and it's going on in there.

GARY: All right then.

MILL: I'd rather look.

GARY [with disgust]: Rather look! She'd rather look, and a bottle of sauce she wants on the table.

MILL: I paid for that, out of my money I paid.

GARY: But where's your money now? Go on, where is it now? Because you won't be told. I'll tell you, never mind other blokes, I'll tell you. A thing or two I'll tell you.

MILL: I'll get something else.

GARY: When? Eh? When? And where?

MILL: There's the Asylum, they use cleaners.

GARY: Not you, they've had you once.

MILL: It was that Matron kept picking on me.

GARY: Has she got her cards? Not her, she won't have you back.

MILL: There's always somewhere.

GARY: And what about next week's money? We're owing rent.

MILL: Haven't you got any?

GARY: I've got what I've got, that's not the point. You can tell that to your Ma. I know, I know, I've heard her. 'Why doesn't he work regular?' Do you think I don't work? Do you?

MILL: I never said . . .

GARY: Never said, oh no, never said, but listen to your Ma say it. Regular! Regular! Like your old man I suppose, knowing every week for forty years what was coming in next week and it wouldn't be enough, and he'd go on cleaning out ditches for the Council till he dropped dead, which he did, unless he won the pools, which he didn't. Did you ever think how it must have been when he first started? There he was, got a job, got a wage, got a wife and that was all he was ever going to have. That was all he ever did have except for six like you, the poor old sod.

MILL: He did his best for us.

GARY: Was that his best?

MILL: They never locked him up.

GARY: You leave my Mum out of it.

MILL: I never said no names.

GARY: Never said, but you meant, I know what you meant.

MILL: What did I mean then?

GARY: Ah shut up, you know, shut up, that's all.

MILL: Tell me what I meant.

GARY: Shut up and go to sleep. Shut up.

[*Another train is heard on the incline, as it fades there is another more sudden and more alarming sound, a kind of squashy thump outside. A long, rustling, scraping noise.*]

MILL [*gives a cry of alarm*]: What's that? On the roof, listen!

GARY: Rats. Old What's-it, old Thurle's hens, he gives them corn, they go for it.

MILL: It wasn't, I know rats.

GARY: They go for it from the dump. That's where they live.

MILL: But something's there. [*Pause.*]

GARY: Not there now.

MILL: It was.

GARY: Ah shut up.

MILL: I'll have a look.

[*Bedsprings creak as she gets out.*]

GARY: This bed, like a Welsh Harp.

[MILL *begins to scream off. Not very loudly, a thin, breathy sound, more like a series of squeaky gasps.*]

GARY: Now what? For Christ's sake what?

MILL [*off*]: Can't see out of the window, something out there, can't see out. We're buried, can't see out.

GARY: Because it's dark.

MILL [*going*]: Something there. Something moving. Quick!

[*Her voice and cries fade as she moves into another room. The bed-springs twang loudly as* GARY *gets up.*]

GARY: Here . . . put a light on.

MILL [*distant*]: Where's the door?

GARY: Light.

MILL: Door door door.

[*Click of switch.*]

GARY: What are you doing then, standing there like that? Put something on.

MILL [*off*]: Dogs, listen to them; dogs.

[*Frantic barking can be heard, every dog in the district.*]

GARY: It's a fox come over the line from the wood, sets them all off. Come on.

MILL [*off*]: If it's that old man hanging round again . . . you get back to bed, I'll give him an eyeful this time. Eyeful of fist.

[*Door off is flung open and* GARY *gasps.*]

MILL [*whimpering*]: Gary . . . Oh Gary . . .

GARY: Shut up! [*Pause.*] What is it though?

MILL [*approach*]: I don't like it.

GARY: Some sort of sheet over the door. Over the . . . yes, over the windows?

MILL: I said . . .

GARY: Shut up what you said. Put something on. Throw my trousers over.

MILL: It moved! I saw where it moved!

GARY: The wind, that's all, it's nothing, only a sheet. Some joke or other. Where are my trousers?

MILL [*off*]: Who?

GARY: What who?

MILL: A joke, who?

GARY: Why would I know? Soon find out though.

[*Ripping of material as* GARY *tears his way out. Calling angrily.*]

Who's there? There's someone. Who are you there?

MILL [*off*]: Gary. . . !

GARY: Come on, who's that, what do you want?

THURLE [*approach. Mildly*]: It's only me, John Thurle.

GARY: I thought it was, I thought! Dirty filthy old man, snooping again. I've got you this time.

THURLE: No no no. I heard a noise.

GARY: Made a noise, that's what you did. Made a noise.

THURLE: Look at your roof. Look! Could I have done that?

GARY [*stunned*]: What is it?

THURLE: That's what I came across to find out, the noise and then my hens and the dogs, I came over.

GARY: Yes, but what is it?

MILL [*off*]: Gary!

GARY: Where are you?

THURLE: Ah good evening my dear. Your husband and I were discussing the phenomenon which has appeared on the roof of your house.

MILL [*approach*]: Not really a house, more of a chalet.

THURLE: On the roof of your dwelling, your simple dwelling.

GARY: But what is it?

THURLE: A parachute I fancy.

MILL: But it's all over everywhere.

THURLE: A very large parachute.

GARY: Yeah, yeah, that's right.

MILL: But how did it come?

THURLE: Out of the sky in the manner of such things.

GARY: What's on the other end?

THURLE: That will be at the back, should we go and look?

MILL: My Mum said once, when it was Battle of Britain, there was a German came down in the garden right next door, and they gave him tea.

GARY [*going*]: Oh come on.

[*Footsteps of three people outdoors.*]

MILL: They said he was nice. Spoke English and everything.

GARY: This way then, mind the van.

MILL: Lucky there's a moon or we wouldn't see.

THURLE: 'The inconstant moon that tips with silver all the fruit-tree tops.' After you my dear.

[*A train approaches drowning all sound. It fades away into the distance before they speak again. The footsteps have stopped.*]

MILL: It's not a chap at all. What is it?

GARY: 'Course it wouldn't be a chap with a parachute that size. I knew that.

MILL: But what is it?

THURLE: Speaking from limited knowledge, my dear, the only newspapers that I study being those used for wrapping my small purchases, I would say that you are looking at what I believe they call, yes . . . a space capsule.

GARY [gives a grunt which is a mixture of disbelief and grudging assent].

MILL: How's it come here?

THURLE: Fallen, fallen like Lucifer, they all come down somewhere. Aren't you cold in that light dress, my dear? You mustn't get cold.

GARY: You leave her alone.

MILL: He wasn't doing anything. Asked if I was cold. I am.

GARY: Well go back in, then. What's it want to land here for?

THURLE: I doubt if it does. In my humble opinion something has gone wrong.

GARY: Could have been dangerous.

MILL: What ought we to do?

GARY: Get the parachute off our roof for a start.

THURLE: First things first, yes.

GARY: Come on then, give a pull at it.

[A train passes.]

GARY: There's some good stuff here.

THURLE: Nothing but the best in the cause of science.

MILL: We ought to tell someone.

GARY: Who?

THURLE: Ah, who?

MILL: Ring up and tell.

GARY: The coppers? We don't want them round.

MILL: I'm getting cold.

GARY: Well go on in then, I said.

MILL: But what are you going to do?

GARY: There's good stuff there in that parachute; and what's the other thing made of?

THURLE: Rare metals I don't doubt.

GARY: Yeah.

MILL: I think we should tell someone.

GARY: Tell the coppers and you know what, they'll be all round poking into everything, probably say I pinched it. They'll book you for anything, give them half a chance.

THURLE: And of course you can never tell what other little irregularities they mightn't discover.

MILL: Gary's all right.

GARY: And what about you? Don't come it on me. I know why you're not a teacher any more.

THURLE: I'm still capable of giving instruction.

GARY: We don't want it, not your sort, not here.

THURLE: We would presume to instruct Daphnis and Chloe? [*He sniggers.*]

MILL: But what about the thing? We can't just leave it, we must tell someone.

THURLE: The Press I fancy would be interested.

GARY: Who?

THURLE: The newspapers. This is news.

GARY: Would they pay?

THURLE: For an exclusive story, certainly.

MILL: What's that?

THURLE: If you telephone one paper and tell them that you have a satellite in your garden you can make your own terms before you give them the address.

GARY: Yeah, telephone, yeah.

THURLE: The nearest box is outside the sweetshop.

GARY: I know that. If you go on up there, Mill, we'll keep an eye.

MILL: I'm not good on the phone.

GARY: Lift it up and ask and put the money in when they say.

MILL: I can't make out what they say.

GARY [*makes a sound of disgust*].

THURLE: Should I go?

MILL: Yes, let him go, Gary, let him, he'll do it best.

GARY: Do it best! Think I can't telephone?

MILL: Yes, but Mr er . . .

THURLE: Thurle.

MILL: He'll know who to ask for.

GARY: I know who to ask for. Think we're all dead ignorant like you?

THURLE: I'll willingly be of any assistance I can.

MILL: He talks proper.

GARY: What's it matter how you talk? It's what you say.

THURLE: Of course. How true.

GARY: And I know what to say.

THURLE: We will keep guard.

GARY: You can do what you like. You go indoors, Mill.

MILL: I'm all right.

GARY: You said you was cold, go on in and stay there, go on.

[*Woman's footsteps going. Door opens and shuts.*]

[*Going:*] I'll take the van, be back before you know.

THURLE: I will keep guard, don't worry.

GARY [*off*]: I'm not worried.

[*The van starts and drives off. There is a slight pause then tapping on a window pane. A window opened.*]

MILL: Yes, what?

THURLE: Do you know something my dear? I too am cold.

[*Cut to coins falling inside a call-box on the pressing of button A.*]

GARY: Hullo . . . hullo. I've got some news. I want to speak to some-one.

OPERATOR [*distort*]: What number are you calling?

GARY: I want to speak to someone. I've got something important.

OPERATOR: What number are you calling?

GARY: I've got a thing . . . a, you know . . . one of them things. Landed back of my place.

OPERATOR: Where are you calling from?

GARY: They said you'd pay for the news, is that right?

OPERATOR: What is the number of the call-box, please?

GARY: I don't tell you that till you say what you'll pay. Did you get me? I've got this thing come down on a parachute and if you want to put it in your paper I'll tell you where to come, only you've got to pay me.

OPERATOR: This is the exchange. What number were you calling?

[*Pause. Fade in the van approaching off.*]

MILL [*in a panic*]: That's the van, that's him coming back, that's Gary.

THURLE: I wouldn't want him to think that I had deserted my post.

MILL: Do hurry, he gets angry.

[*Door opens.*]

THURLE: Do you like milk chocolate?

MILL: Yes; do hurry though, please.

THURLE: What have I here? A sixpenny bar, and half of it for you.
[*The crisp snap of a bar of chocolate.*]

MILL: Oh thanks, but here he is.
[*Door shuts as the van drives up and stops. Door of the van slams.*]

THURLE: Ah, what luck, Daphnis?

GARY [*off*]: Who?

THURLE: A joke, a little joke. What luck?

GARY [*approach*]: Waste of time.

THURLE: Oh dear, didn't you get through?

GARY: I got through all right, got through yes.

THURLE: They didn't believe you?

GARY: I couldn't get no sense out of them, stupid they were. Half asleep I reckon.

THURLE: Tst. What a way to run a newspaper.
[*Door opens off.*]

MILL [*off*]: Is it all right, Gary?

GARY: What do you mean, all right? I'm all right.

THURLE: The problem is still on your hands.

MILL [*approach*]: Are they giving us money?

GARY: They're dopey, they don't know what time it is.

THURLE: Two little thoughts have entered my head while you were away.

GARY: Dirty ones, I bet.

MILL: Gary!

GARY: All right, well what?

THURLE: First we should consider the possibility that this object may have an occupant.

GARY: Eh?

THURLE: Someone in it.

MILL: In there?

THURLE: Possibly.

MILL: Oh, poor chap.

GARY: There wouldn't be.

THURLE: There has been in the past, there will be in the future, so why not now?
[*Knuckles rapping on hard surface.*]

GARY: It don't even sound hollow.

THURLE: Ah but if you come round this side you will see that there is something which appears to be a hatch-cover.

GARY: All bolted on.

THURLE: Naturally; they wouldn't want it to come open by accident, and if you come round here where it's tilted over, you will see what appears to be a window.

GARY: Here, here, let's have a look then.

THURLE: My old bones wouldn't let me down there, I thought it best to wait for youth.

MILL: See anything, Gary?

GARY [*slightly off, grunting a bit*]: It's awkward, got to keep your head down . . . no don't see nothing. All dark.

THURLE: Unconscious possibly.

GARY: I got an adjustable might undo those bolts.

THURLE: Very unwise, if I may say so.

MILL: We've got to get him out, can't leave him there, I mean.

THURLE: Assuming that he's in there.

GARY [*approach*]: You said he was.

THURLE: No no, might be, that's all I said, might be.

MILL: Nobody's come out.

THURLE: There may be nobody to come out; or a dog or a monkey or a rat.

GARY: You mean nothing in there only machinery and that?

THURLE: That's what I mean.

GARY: We'll have a look then.

THURLE: No wait. If . . . and remember that I say if, I make no definite statement; if it is unmanned then it is more than possible that its builders have provided for its destruction in the event of it falling into the wrong hands.

GARY: Say what you mean.

THURLE: It might blow up if you interfered with it.

GARY: Blow up? That. Why should it blow up?

MILL: Oh, Gary, yes. Like they put notices on the Heath after those kids was killed playing with a bomb.

[GARY *makes a scornful noise.*]

There was! And the police said not to pick up objects.

GARY: Wanted it left for them in case there was stuff they could flog. Bring the spanner.

THURLE: Wait.

GARY: You don't like it, you go home. I want to see what's there.

THURLE: It may deprive you of a considerable sum of money.

GARY: How's that?

THURLE: I've had another little thought.

GARY: Well?

THURLE: We elderly gentlemen find the night air cold. Supposing we were to enter your dwelling.

MILL: Yes, Gary, let's go in.

GARY: I got ideas of my own, I don't need his help.

THURLE: You are thinking perhaps of selling the parachute material, for a start.

GARY: It's in my garden, counts as mine.

THURLE: You can do much much better than that. There's a great deal of money involved.

GARY: A great deal of talk.

MILL: Oh, Gary, do listen. He does know.

THURLE: Thank you, my dear.

GARY: I know what he knows.

MILL: You don't.

GARY: What's that mean?

MILL [too quickly]: He's been a teacher, he knows things.

GARY [going]: Oh all right, but we're not going to sit round rabbiting all night.

[Footsteps of three people outdoors. Change to interior acoustic as they go inside. Footsteps stop. Door closes.]

[Approach.] There's good stuff in that parachute. I don't need teaching that.

THURLE [approach]: Charming, quite charming, a little love nest.

GARY: You say what you've got to.

MILL [approach]: Suppose we sit, you know – sit down: that bus seat there's the best. Shall I get cocoa?

GARY: Shut up, let's hear.

THURLE: You have out there an article of considerable value to certain people.

GARY: Value to me, that's what matters.

THURLE: There are three groups who would be very interested in it. Group A being our own dear Government.

GARY: Well?

THURLE: If you inform them they will come along and take it away and that will probably be that.

MILL: But there'd be something to come from the papers.

THURLE: I doubt it very much, it will become an Official Secret.

GARY: Well then, well? Go on.

THURLE: We can say for certain that our dear Government are not the builders of this object, and sad it is to say.

GARY: Who is?

THURLE: Either Group B, as we will call our friends across the Atlantic, or Group C, the others.

MILL: Germans?

GARY: Russians, not Germans, Russians: that's what he means.

THURLE: Yes. Think how much they must want their plaything back.

[*Pause.*]

GARY: We don't know which.

THURLE: No.

MILL: Perhaps there's writing on it.

GARY [*scornfully*]: Writing! Get out.

MILL: Russian writing's different.

THURLE: It doesn't matter either way.

GARY: How's that?

THURLE: Whichever group it belongs to, the other group will be even more eager to see it.

GARY: Yeah, yeah, I get you, yeah.

MILL: How does he mean?

GARY: Sort of spies.

THURLE: Correct.

GARY: How would we kind of get in touch?

THURLE: One would telephone the Embassy in question and make an appointment to meet in some discreet spot.

GARY: Yeah. [*He sounds doubtful.*]

THURLE: I would do the telephoning if you liked.

GARY: I can do it.

MILL: Oh let him, Gary, he'll know better what to say.

GARY: Who says he will? Think I don't know what to say?

THURLE: Of course you do, but if I can help you naturally I shall be delighted.

GARY: And to take the money.

MILL: Oh, Gary.

THURLE: Some of the money, yes, why not?

GARY: That's all it is, you see.

THURLE: I don't think that we should let it go for less than ten thousand pounds.

GARY: Ten thousand?

THURLE: It has cost several million to put it where it is, we might get more if we played our cards properly. I would suggest splitting it three ways.

GARY: That'd be . . . that'd be . . .

THURLE: Three thousand, three hundred and thirty-three pounds, six shillings and eightpence each.

MILL: Is it?

GARY: That's a hell of a lot less than ten thousand.

THURLE: As man and wife your combined share comes to six thousand, six hundred and sixty pounds, thirteen shillings and fourpence.

GARY [*makes a non-committal sound*].

MILL: It's a whole lot, Gary.

GARY: What'll they give us? I mean how'll it come?

THURLE: In cash, we shall demand cash; five-pound notes.

MILL: We won't know where to put them. We won't!

GARY: We could take dollars, sell it to the Yanks, they'd give us dollars, best to sell it to the Yanks anyway, they've got the money.

THURLE [*doubtfully*]: Possibly, possibly, possibly.

GARY: Well?

THURLE: We have no exact means of knowing how they will react.

MILL: They're smart, Yanks are, they'll know what's best.

GARY: Loud-mouthed big talkers, that's all.

THURLE: They just might consider it their duty to inform our Government.

GARY: And then what?

THURLE: Then again we'd get nothing.

GARY: And you, big talk too. Ten thousand you said, now you say nothing. Which way is it?

MILL: He's only saying what might happen.

GARY: He said they'd pay, now he says they won't pay.

THURLE: One has to look at this from every angle, every angle.

GARY: I want an angle that's got some lolly in it. If you want to look at any others you can push off back to your hen-house.

THURLE: Very well then, this is my humble suggestion, that we should approach Group C first.

MILL: Which lot's that?

THURLE: The Other lot my dear. We should approach them and see what they are prepared to pay. If it's inadequate we approach Group B.

GARY: You said notes, five-pound notes.

THURLE: Yes.

GARY: Now you say in addy something, what's that?

THURLE: Inadequate.

MILL: Not enough.

GARY: I know, I know, just didn't hear. All right.

THURLE: Not enough, as you say, my dear. In this way we will have a better chance of testing out both sides. You see the Russians will be unable to prevent us contacting the Americans, but they might very well prevent us from contacting the Russians.

GARY: Why?

THURLE: It's a little late to discuss the current political situation.

MILL: The Yanks are on our side and the Russians aren't.

THURLE: Brilliant, my dear, as clever as you're charming.

GARY: They'd be foreigners.

THURLE: They're all foreigners.

GARY: Yeah, but . . .

MILL: Them other lot are more foreign.

THURLE: Their money is the same. [*Pause.*] We should act without undue delay.

GARY: What, telephone now?

THURLE: If you had a shilling or two to spare I would go up to the box.

GARY: There, that's it! Listen to him. On the scrounge for a bob. I knew.

MILL: But if he's telephoning . . .

GARY: How do you know what he'll do?

THURLE: If you care to drive me up to the box you could witness my call.

GARY: There'll be no one there now.

THURLE: Oh, I'm sure they never sleep.

GARY: Well, I don't know . . .

MILL: What, Gary?

GARY: That lot, foreign, you don't know where you are.

THURLE: They'll pay and they'll keep quiet, for their own sakes.

GARY: Yeah, I know, but . . . all the same . . .

MILL: They're not on our side.

THURLE: Do you imagine, seriously imagine, that anyone is on your side? Have they ever been? Of course they haven't. Look where you live and how you live. Does anyone care? Oh no no no, they look down on you from the trains, they see the muddy pools and the cinder track and the council dump at the end of it; they don't notice you, why should they? If there wasn't a rubbish dump there wouldn't even be a road to your door.

GARY [*sulkily*]: I'd make one.

THURLE: Oh no my dear boy, no, they wouldn't let you, don't you understand? Everyone's against you. Take what you can from them before they put you on the dump with the broken prams and the rusty stoves, that's what they'd like to do, me too. We don't belong.

GARY: I've never been in your sort of trouble, never would neither.

THURLE: Once you're inside a Police Station you don't know what trouble you'll find yourself in.

MILL: You say that Gary.

GARY: My kind of bloke, not his, they like his sort, wouldn't nail them 'less they had to.

THURLE: When I was in there, do you know? When I was there being questioned, they told me to sit down. 'Sit down,' they said and gave me a push so that I sat on the stove. They laughed.

GARY [*laughs loudly*].

MILL: Oh, Gary . . .

GARY: Old hot pants! [*He laughs again.*]

THURLE: Yes, funny in a way, I agree, oh yes, but they can be just as nasty to anyone; you.

MILL: That's right.

THURLE: And Group B are on their side.

GARY: Don't the other lot have coppers then?

THURLE: None that are interested in you.

GARY: All the same I . . . Well it's all right talking and it's all right for you, but . . .

THURLE: Your patriotism does you credit.

GARY [*with a derisive sound*]: It's not that.

MILL [*eating*]: We had ought to decide.

GARY: Here! What are you eating there? You eating chocolate?

MILL: Yeah, milk.

GARY: Where'd you get that?

MILL: Had it by me.

GARY: You never! I know what you got by you, and there wasn't no chocolate.

THURLE: Look . . .

GARY: He give it you, didn't he? When I went off. That right? You give it her?

THURLE: I . . .

GARY: Yes you did, I might have known, you come in here when I went off.

MILL: Why shouldn't he?

GARY: There, he did, I know and you let him in you did!

MILL: Said he was cold.

GARY: Old hot pants cold! You dirty old, filthy old, mucky old . . . I know you, I do know you and teach you I will.

MILL: No, leave him.

GARY: You leave him.

[*There is a cry from* MILL *as she stumbles and falls from a push.*]

As bad as him.

THURLE: No . . .

GARY: Let you have it . . . [*A blow*].

THURLE: No, please . . . !

GARY: Come in here . . . [*another blow*] . . . my wife . . . [*again a blow*].

THURLE: Don't! Oh no, don't!

MILL: You'll kill him, Gary.

GARY: Not me, not this time. Had enough.

THURLE [*sobbing*]: I . . . let me go . . .

GARY: Get on.

[*Door open.*]

Get on then, out!

[THURLE, *still sobbing, goes out to the sound of a parting kick.* GARY *calls after him.*]

And stick to school kids next time!

[*Door slam. He gives a sigh, almost of contentment. A job well done.* MILL *is snuffling.*]

MILL [*off*]: You shouldn't have . . .

GARY: And you let him in.

MILL [*approach*]: He never did nothing.

[GARY *makes a noise of contempt.*]
   No. He tried to.
GARY: What?
MILL: Well nothing much, but tried. I told him no.
GARY: Yeah, and then you sat around until I come back?
MILL: He talked.
GARY: Yeah!
MILL: Sort of stuff about how beautiful love was, and some Indian
   book: and how it was supposed to make us better but wouldn't if
   we didn't understand it.
GARY: Dirty talk?
MILL [*going*]: No, he didn't say nothing, just talk.
GARY: All he's up to.
MILL [*off*]: Look, there's blood there where you hit him.
GARY: Do him good to lose a bit.
MILL: I'll rub it off, it'll make marks.
   [*There is a sharp explosion outside.*]
   [*Gives a cry.*] What's that? Is it him come back? He's got a gun.
GARY: No, that's no gun.
MILL [*approach*]: It is, it's him. He's come back to shoot us, I know he
   is . . . !
GARY: Shut up, it's that thing.
MILL: Blown up! He said it would.
GARY: There'd be more than that if it blew up. [*Going.*] I'll take a
   look.
   [*Door open off.*]
MILL: Don't touch it, Gary. [*Going.*] Let's get someone who knows.
   [*Outdoor acoustic.*]
GARY [*approach*]: Here, Mill, here.
MILL [*off*]: What is it?
GARY: Here, come here.
MILL [*approach*]: What's happened then?
GARY: That hatch thing's blown itself off.
MILL: Don't go too near.
GARY: It's okay. There's a light inside.
MILL: Is there someone in there?
GARY: Hullo! Anyone? [*His voice changes as he puts his head inside.*]
   Anyone? Nobody. Lots of things though.
MILL: Do come out.

GARY: No, come on and look, it's all right, nothing to bite you, there's all sorts here. Look at that.

MILL [*incredulous*]: That's a flower!

GARY: And all sorts, look at them dials.

MILL: No, but a flower. Who'd put a flower in there and send it up?

GARY: Look here then though, there's eggs, ten eggs, all packed careful.

MILL: It's a joke, someone's having us on.

GARY: No, don't talk soft, how could they? Who?

MILL: He's got eggs, old Thing.

GARY: And he'd give us ten for a joke? Not him. No, I tell you what this is; this is scientific, all sort of experiments. Look at them bottles and things, and seeds, look there's all kinds of seeds, in jars.

MILL: Oh, we ought to tell someone.

GARY: See what there is first. Here, you take the flower.

MILL: It's growing in water, with roots and all.

GARY: Put it down then. Careful.

MILL: Sort of like a daisy, only big.

GARY: Now the eggs, they'll do us.

MILL [*giggles*]: Eggs.

GARY: What's the giggle then?

MILL: Suppose I dropped them?

GARY: Don't.

MILL: But they have been dropped, that's what's funny.

GARY: Here, take these jars.

MILL: What are they?

GARY: Sort of seeds and things. It don't matter what they are, the jars are good. I know who'll give tuppence each for these empty, more for the big ones. It's all profit this. Here, look what we got here.

MILL: What's that?

GARY: Look.

MILL: Potatoes!

GARY: Yeah, ten, same as the eggs. Ordinary spuds. I'll tell you what. [*He begins to laugh.*] Tell you what, Mill, what we'll have, we'll have egg and chips.

MILL: Egg and chips!

GARY: Sent down from heaven, answer to a prayer. 'Oh, God, send us egg and chips.' 'Egg and chips twice coming down.'

MILL [*laughing*]: Oh, Gary, you are . . .

GARY: Here, you take them in and start peeling, I'll get the rest out.

MILL [*savouring the joke*]: 'Coming down twice.'

GARY: There's a big jar down here, all sort of connected up; kind of rum jar, that'd be a laugh.

[*Suddenly a harsh mechanical voice begins to speak. It is impossible to tell its nationality.*]

VOICE: Do not touch.

MILL [*gives a scream*].

[*The voice continues. It says 'Do not touch' in various languages.* MILL *and* GARY *drop their voices, and move slightly away from the machine.*]

MILL: Where is he?

GARY: Not in there, couldn't be.

MILL: But he's talking.

GARY: Radio, that's what. Talking on a radio.

[*The voice stops.*]

MILL: But where?

GARY: How do I know where it come from.

MILL: It gave me a fright.

GARY: It's nothing.

MILL: No, Gary, don't, best not go near again.

GARY: Not go near?

MILL: He said.

GARY: He can't do nothing. He's not here.

MILL: But he knew you was touching.

[*The voice starts again, repeating exactly the same words as before. Their heads are inside again.*]

GARY: I'll tell you what that is. It's a tape that's all, touch the top of that jar and it starts up.

MILL: It says not touch.

GARY: Yeah, it says, but it don't know nothing. Look here's where it comes from.

MILL: Comes from there?

GARY: On a tape, that's all. Automatic. Shut up!

[*There is the sound of a blow and the voice stops.*]

Fixed him.

MILL: Oh, Gary, you shouldn't have.

GARY: Trying to keep us off the old rum jar.

MILL: There's a little light in it.

GARY: I'll get it out, have a proper look.
   [*Sounds of effort.*]

MILL: There's something in there.

GARY: I didn't think it was empty, did I?

MILL: Some sort of fish, look – floating.

GARY: Eh?

MILL: There, when it steadies, look. It's like a fish sort of, got kind of little arms, kind of little legs, all hunched up. Do you see? And it's alive, look where its heart's beating! Funny sort of thing.

GARY [*low but very intense*]: Shut up!

MILL: No, but look at it, Gary.

GARY: Shut up will you! Come away.
   [*They move away from the machine to an outdoor acoustic.*]

MILL: But Gary . . .

GARY: Come on in.

MILL: But all the stuff.

GARY: Come on.

MILL: The eggs.

GARY: Leave them. [*Going.*] Leave the lot, come on in.

MILL [*going*]: Gary, what's the matter?
   [*Door slams. They are now inside.*]
 [*Approach.*] What is it?

GARY [*approach*]: What's what?

MILL: The matter with you? All that stuff and the eggs and them potatoes, and now you say leave it.

GARY: Yeah.

MILL: But we can't just leave it now. Someone will see, they'll want to know.

GARY: There's a tarpaulin in the van, sling that over it.

MILL: I can't do that alone. Why not you?

GARY: Wait, all right, but wait.

MILL: If you'd tell me.

GARY: Tell you! Don't you know what that was?

MILL: That little fish thing?

GARY: That, yeah. I know what it was, seen one before.

MILL: What then?

GARY: When I was a kid. Found it one day, wrapped up out where we put the rubbish. Didn't know what it was then. Got a walloping from Mum for being nosy.

MILL: Well?

GARY: You know about her.

MILL: Your Mum?

GARY: What they booked her for. What they put her inside over.

MILL: Yeah, I know that. There was a woman down our road doing it too.

GARY: Then you know what's in that jar.

MILL: Oh no, Gary! No! It couldn't be.

GARY: Bloody well is.

MILL: But what for? Who'd do that?

GARY: Shut up about it.

MILL: Yes, but who would? I mean . . .

GARY [*cutting in*]: Drop it! I said shut up. I don't know who would or why they would or who they are. Just let it be, that's all.

MILL [*going*]: I'll get that tarpaulin then.
[*A train approaches, clanks up the incline, whistles and moves slowly off into the distance. Pause. Door opens off.*]

MILL [*approach*]: Gary . . . Gary . . . I've done what I could, like you said.

GARY: What's that?

MILL: Put the tarpaulin over, but I can't get it over proper, I can't reach. And, Gary, you know that jar?

GARY: Well?

MILL: It got knocked over. Them wires were broke and some of the stuff came out . . .

GARY: And?

MILL: And it wasn't moving any more. I put it out.

GARY: Where?

MILL: Took it along to the dump, slung it.

GARY: And the jar?

MILL: I thought that best.

GARY: Yeah . . . yeah, that's best. [*There is relief in his voice.*]

MILL: And those eggs, you know those eggs, I trod on one. They aren't no good, they wouldn't be nice.

GARY: No, I knew they wouldn't be.

MILL: Like some cocoa?

GARY: Wouldn't mind.

MILL: There's the tarpaulin.

GARY: I know, I know, I'll do that.

MILL: And all that stuff.

GARY: We'll sling all that.

MILL: Worth money, you said.

GARY: We'll get enough without the jars. All them dials and that electric stuff, I'll have that out. There's a bloke runs a stall down the market. Gives a good price for that stuff, anything electrical. Then I'll get on to Ted. He can get hold of a welding set so we can get the other thing carved up and took across the Common.

MILL: He'll want paying for that.

GARY: He can come in on it. There's good stuff there, and the parachute. We'll make fifty quid all told.

MILL: Fifty!

GARY: Maybe more. What you want to do?

MILL: Do?

GARY: I'll take you out somewhere, give you a good time. Or you could buy something. Or what you liked. Only have to say.

MILL: Only really?

GARY: Yeah.

MILL: Because I know, I do know.

GARY: What you want? Right then, say.

MILL: It's what you didn't want. What you said there wasn't any point us having, and we wouldn't know what to do with it, and there was too many people as it was.

GARY: And now you want one?

MILL: Yes.

GARY: Why?

MILL: Out there on the dump with that thing I was thinking. I could see, when you'd told me what it was, and there was an old rat sitting on a bit of box and waiting till I went. They're clever all that lot.

GARY: Rats are?

MILL: All that lot, clever. Make a thing like that and put things in it and send it up. You'd never think anyone could be that clever. He knew I'd be gone soon and he'd get it. But we can beat 'em all. And the old man.

GARY: Him? Why him?

MILL: All his talk. He's clever, not like us, but . . .

46

GARY: Yeah – okay then. Yeah – we will. [*He laughs.*] What'll we call it?

MILL: Early days yet. See what it is first.

GARY [*softly*]: Early? Is it early? All that early?

MILL [*giggling*]: No, Gary, no . . .

GARY: You said.

MILL: You won't get no cocoa. Don't you want some?

GARY: All right. [*Going.*] I'll put that tarpaulin on proper.

MILL [*voice louder*]: What about them beans?

GARY [*off*]: What?

MILL: Do you want the rest of them beans?

GARY [*off*]: Might as well. Got to keep my strength up now.

MILL: Awful, you are.

GARY: Awful, yes. Oh, Mill!

MILL: Hullo?

GARY [*closer*]: Keep the tin.

MILL: What?

GARY: That tin, keep it, like I said. There's no point wasting nothing.
[*Another train begins to approach.* MILL *begins to sing – any pop song will do. Her voice can be heard above the sound of the train. Fade.*]

END

BARRY BERMANGE

No Quarter

No Quarter was first broadcast on the B.B.C. Third Programme on 14 November 1962 with the following cast:

LANDLORD	Peter Pratt
FAT MAN	Felix Felton
QUIET MAN	Denys Hawthorne
MILITARY MAN	Carleton Hobbs

Produced by John Gibson

THE HOTEL

Total darkness. The LANDLORD, *the* FAT MAN, *and the* QUIET MAN *climbing stairs. The* LANDLORD *is one flight ahead. They have reached the fifteenth landing. The* FAT MAN *cries out irritably.*

FAT MAN: How much farther are you taking us!

LANDLORD: Not far to go now, sir.

FAT MAN: We must be nearing the roof!

LANDLORD: Oh that. No. The next landing will see us there.

FAT MAN: You said that nine landings ago.

LANDLORD: It's a big hotel, sir. One tends to lose one's bearings.

FAT MAN: One tends to get cold, too, at such an altitude.

LANDLORD: Yes, I'm sorry about that.

FAT MAN: I suppose your boilers aren't working.

LANDLORD: There's been a complication, sir. I'm expecting the man tomorrow.

FAT MAN: Of all the luck. The only hotel for miles and nothing works in it. No light! No heat! Nothing! Ah! [*In pain.*]

LANDLORD [*stopping*]: Something wrong, sir?

FAT MAN: My knee . . .

LANDLORD: What about it?

FAT MAN: I've knocked it.

LANDLORD: Not on the banister.

FAT MAN: Where else!

LANDLORD: That's twice you've knocked your knee on the banister.

FAT MAN: I know! You don't have to remind me! Ah!

LANDLORD: Stone a crow. You've done it again.

FAT MAN: Don't just stand there. *Do* something.

LANDLORD: What?

FAT MAN: Turn on a light! Oh, my knee . . .

LANDLORD: But I've already explained, sir . . .

FAT MAN: My knee . . .

LANDLORD: . . . About the light I mean. We've had a fuse blown. That's the reason for the lamp. Fuses are very temperamental, I might tell you. They blow at the drop of a hat. This one blew just before you came. About a quarter of an hour before. Well, ten minutes.

FAT MAN: My knee . . .

LANDLORD: You see, Mr Barton, sir, we're on one of them circuits where if one light goes they all go, every last one of them. Well, the one in the kitchen went – or was it the hall? – no, no, it was the kitchen one, the kitchen one. Well, the kitchen one went and the others went with it.

FAT MAN: I don't care . . . just get me to my room.

[*Pause.*]

Our room. Get us to *our* room and be quick about it.

LANDLORD: Follow me, sir. [*He climbs.*]

FAT MAN: And don't hold that lamp so low. We're almost in darkness down here. [*He climbs. The* QUIET MAN *follows.*]

LANDLORD: That better, sir?

FAT MAN [*groaning*]: These cases, these cases . . .

QUIET MAN: May I carry one for you, Mr Barton?

FAT MAN: What!

QUIET MAN: One of your cases, Mr Barton.

FAT MAN: Thank you. I'll manage . . .

QUIET MAN: It would be no trouble, Mr Barton.

FAT MAN: I'd rather you didn't . . .

QUIET MAN: I'd be very very careful with it, Mr Barton. I would take very very special care not to knock it or anything.

FAT MAN: Please, it's all right . . .

QUIET MAN: Very well, Mr Barton. You know best. But it seems unfair that a man of your age should carry three big cases up all these stairs while a man of my age carries none. Apart from this, it would give me very very great pleasure to carry one or even two . . . for you. Now what do you say?

LANDLORD [*calling down*]: Well, sir?

FAT MAN: What . . .

LANDLORD [*louder*]: Mr Barton, sir!

FAT MAN: What . . . what!

LANDLORD: I asked if that was better, sir.

FAT MAN: Better?

QUIET MAN: He is referring to the lamp, Mr Barton. Look. He is holding it higher now.

FAT MAN: Oh . . . yes . . . [*Calling up*]. Yes, that's all right now!

[*They climb in silence for a moment.*]

QUIET MAN: Well, Mr Barton?

FAT MAN: Well what?

QUIET MAN: About the cases.

FAT MAN: I've told you. No!

QUIET MAN: I asked again because I thought you might have changed your mind.

FAT MAN: Well I haven't.

QUIET MAN: You'd rather carry them yourself?

FAT MAN: Yes. I need no help. I can manage quite adequately on my own . . .

> [*They continue climbing, the* FAT MAN *struggling with his cases. Fade. Silence.*]

LANDLORD: Here we are, gents.

> [*The* FAT MAN *and the* QUIET MAN *join him. We hear the* FAT MAN *panting. Hold under in background.*]

QUIET MAN: Quite a climb, Mr Binks.

LANDLORD: One gets used to it.

QUIET MAN: Perhaps one day you will install a lift.

LANDLORD [*after a pause*]: I've got a lift. [*Pause.*] It's out of order. [*Pause.*] Oh yes. I've got a lift. You need a lift in a place this size. But it's out of order. Trouble with the counterweight. Yes. The counterweight. Been out of order for months. [*Pause.*] Counterweight trouble.

QUIET MAN: Can't you get it repaired?

LANDLORD: You think I haven't tried? I've tried all right. God knows I've tried. But do you think I can get it fixed?

QUIET MAN: There must be someone . . . somewhere . . .

LANDLORD: I was recommended to get in touch with a man in Hornsey – know Hornsey do you?

> [*Pause.*]

I must remember to get in touch with him.

> [*The* FAT MAN *begins to pant very loudly.*]

Our friend here seems a bit puffed.

QUIET MAN: The climb. It exhausted him.

LANDLORD: You all right, sir?

FAT MAN [*rapid panting*].

LANDLORD: You should have let him help you with your cases.

> [*A thin whine comes through the panting.*]

When he asked you should have let him. Lugging all that lot up here by yourself . . . why, you might have done yourself an injury.

[*On the word 'injury' the* FAT MAN *stops panting. Stops dead. Pause.*]

FAT MAN: Injury?

LANDLORD: My word he does look queer, doesn't he?

QUIET MAN: He'll be all right.

FAT MAN: Did you say *injury*?

QUIET MAN: A figure of speech, Mr Barton.

LANDLORD: Flushed. Flushed and drawn. Don't you think he looks flushed and drawn?

QUIET MAN: He'll be all right after a good night's sleep.

LANDLORD: You think so?

QUIET MAN: Why not?

LANDLORD: I'd hate there to be any illness in the place.

QUIET MAN: I can assure you, Mr Binks, there is no danger of that.

FAT MAN: Danger?

QUIET MAN: A figure of speech, Mr Barton.

LANDLORD [*laughs*]: That's it. A figure of speech! Nothing to worry about. Come on. Your room's down here. [*Goes.*]
    [*Pause.*]

QUIET MAN: Coming, Mr Barton?

FAT MAN: Just a minute.

QUIET MAN: Yes?

FAT MAN: What was he saying to you?

QUIET MAN: Who?

FAT MAN: Mr Binks.

QUIET MAN: When?

FAT MAN: Just now.

QUIET MAN: What about?

FAT MAN: About danger. And injury.

QUIET MAN: He was just talking, that's all . . .

FAT MAN: What about?

QUIET MAN: Well . . . generally. You know . . . generally?

FAT MAN [*pausing*]: There's nothing going on, is there?

QUIET MAN: Going on?

FAT MAN: You know what I mean. [*Pause.*] Well is there?

QUIET MAN [*pausing*]: He's waiting for us. He's down this corridor. Our room's down here. Coming? [*Going.*] Come on. It's perfectly safe. There's nothing to worry about. Just pick up your cases . . . and follow . . .

[*The* FAT MAN *follows. Fade.*]
[*Silence.*]

LANDLORD: Here we are!

QUIET MAN: Room Number 3 . . . 2 . . . 8 . . . 1.

LANDLORD: That's the one!

FAT MAN: Open up!

QUIET MAN: May we go in?

LANDLORD: It's locked.

QUIET MAN: What?

LANDLORD: Safety Precaution.

QUIET MAN: But you've a key.

LANDLORD: Somewhere. [*Fumbles.*]

FAT MAN: Open up! [*Pause.*] What's keeping him!

QUIET MAN: Ssh . . .

FAT MAN: What's happening?

QUIET MAN: The door of the room is locked.

FAT MAN: Locked!

QUIET MAN: Safety Precaution.

FAT MAN: Hasn't he got a key?

QUIET MAN: He's looking for it now.

LANDLORD: That's funny. I could have sworn I had it on me. It must be here somewhere. Hold the lamp a tick someone . . .

QUIET MAN: Here . . .

LANDLORD: Let me see now . . . [*Fumbles.*]
    [*Pause.*]

QUIET MAN: How high up are we?

LANDLORD: What?

QUIET MAN: Are we very high? Are we . . . in the clouds?
    [*Pause.*]

FAT MAN: Well!

LANDLORD: It must be here somewhere.

QUIET MAN: Perhaps you've mislaid it.

LANDLORD: Can't see how I could have.

QUIET MAN: I have often mislaid keys myself.

LANDLORD: Really?

FAT MAN: Hurry! I'm cold!

LANDLORD: Where is it . . .

FAT MAN: What's the delay!

QUIET MAN: The key. He's still looking for it.

FAT MAN: But I'm freezing!

QUIET MAN: Patience.

LANDLORD [*fumbling sounds*].

QUIET MAN: Which pocket do you usually keep keys in?

LANDLORD: . . . this is the Sixteenth Floor.

QUIET MAN: I'm talking about *keys*. I suppose you've got a special key pocket.

LANDLORD: This one here. This side one here. Down here.

QUIET MAN: And if it isn't in that one?
  [*Pause.*]

LANDLORD: What do you mean?

QUIET MAN: Perhaps, without realizing, you slipped it into another one.

LANDLORD: What!

QUIET MAN: It's possible.

LANDLORD: This is the key pocket. This!

QUIET MAN: But it isn't in there, Mr Binks.

LANDLORD: It must be.

QUIET MAN: Is there a hole in the pocket by any chance?
  [*Pause.*]

LANDLORD: What are you insinuating?

QUIET MAN: Merely that if there *is* a hole in the pocket, the key might have slipped through to the lining – have you searched the lining?

LANDLORD: There isn't . . . a hole.

QUIET MAN: That settles that then, doesn't it?

FAT MAN: Mr Binks! I demand service!

QUIET MAN: He's still looking.

FAT MAN: This is an outrage!

QUIET MAN: Relax, Mr Barton.

FAT MAN: I am tired and I want to go to bed!

QUIET MAN: You will. In good time.

FAT MAN: I want to go now!

QUIET MAN: We can't get in.

FAT MAN: You mean he's *lost* the key?

QUIET MAN: No. But he has yet to find it.

FAT MAN: What about the duplicate?

QUIET MAN [*to the* LANDLORD]: He says what about the duplicate.

LANDLORD: There isn't a duplicate.

FAT MAN: There must be a duplicate.

QUIET MAN: He says there must be a duplicate.

LANDLORD: Well there isn't.

QUIET MAN [*to the* FAT MAN]: There isn't.

FAT MAN [*groans*]: Oh God. I'm so miserable!

QUIET MAN: He says he's miserable.

LANDLORD: I'm doing my best.

QUIET MAN: Look . . . Why not try another pocket?

LANDLORD: *This* is the *key* pocket!

QUIET MAN: It wouldn't hurt to try. Just to make sure?

LANDLORD: No! It wouldn't be in another pocket – it couldn't be –
   I know. I never put keys in them. I put *other* things in them. Wait
   a minute . . .

FAT MAN: Has he found it?

QUIET MAN: You've found it?

LANDLORD: No. But I think I remember where it is. Here. Give me
   the lamp. [*Taking the lamp.*] Yes . . . I think I remember. It's all
   right. Nothing to worry about. It's downstairs. I'll fetch it. [*Going.*]
   You wait here. With him.

   [*We hear the* LANDLORD *descending flights of stairs, his footsteps
   getting fainter as he descends. They fade. Silence.*]

FAT MAN: Where has he gone?

QUIET MAN: *Down* . . .

FAT MAN: Why?

QUIET MAN: For the key. The key to our room.

FAT MAN: Will he be long?

QUIET MAN: He may be a very very short time. And on the other
   hand he may be a very very long time. He may be back in a flash.
   He may never be back.

FAT MAN [*pausing*]: This darkness . . .

QUIET MAN: Does it worry you, Mr Barton?

FAT MAN: No. Why should it?

QUIET MAN: It might.

FAT MAN: It doesn't. Why do you ask?

QUIET MAN: There are many people who are afraid of the dark.
   Are you, Mr Barton?

FAT MAN: Me? Why should I be? I've got nothing to be afraid of.
   [*Pause.*] Are you still there?

QUIET MAN: I am here.

FAT MAN: Be careful. Won't you.

QUIET MAN: Of what?

FAT MAN: The banisters. Whatever you do, don't lean against the banisters. They aren't safe. In fact if I were you I wouldn't move at all. No. I wouldn't move at all if I were you.

    [*Pause.*]

QUIET MAN: We're very very high up, aren't we?

FAT MAN: We are.

QUIET MAN: I thought we were. [*Pause.*] We came up thousands and thousands of stairs, didn't we?

FAT MAN: We did.

QUIET MAN: I tried to count them. I got to nine hundred and seventy-seven. Then you tripped. I lost count when you tripped. How many stairs do you think we climbed, Mr Barton?

FAT MAN: Enough. [*Pause.*] What are you doing?

QUIET MAN: Standing. Standing very very still. I like standing still.

FAT MAN: He should have left the lamp!

QUIET MAN: What for?

FAT MAN: For us! For you and me!

QUIET MAN: He needed it himself.

FAT MAN: We are his guests. We have more right to it than him. Besides, our need for it is greater than his.

QUIET MAN: Is it?

FAT MAN: He knows his way around. Do we?

QUIET MAN: Oh. Yes. Yes I think I know what you mean.

FAT MAN [*suspicious*]: Have you ever been in this hotel before?

QUIET MAN: Have you?

FAT MAN: I'm asking you.

QUIET MAN: It's such a *big* hotel. . . . How high up did you say you thought we were?

FAT MAN: I didn't say.

QUIET MAN: I thought you did. [*Pause.*] What are you doing?

FAT MAN [*pausing*]: What did you say your name was?

QUIET MAN: What?

FAT MAN: Oh . . . nothing.

QUIET MAN: Why don't you stand still. It is nice to stand still.

FAT MAN: This darkness . . . where does it end?

QUIET MAN: The darkness makes us seem higher than perhaps we are. We do *seem* high, don't we? [*Pause.*] Where are you now?

FAT MAN: Still here. I haven't moved.

QUIET MAN: I thought I heard you moving.

FAT MAN: You heard someone moving?

QUIET MAN: I thought it was you. It was probably me. [*Pause.*] Pity about the lift, isn't it?

FAT MAN: *Lift!*

QUIET MAN: Mr Binks's lift.

FAT MAN: He has a *lift!*

QUIET MAN: It's out of order. It's been out of order for months now.

FAT MAN: He might have said.

QUIET MAN: He did say.

FAT MAN: When?

QUIET MAN: You were out of breath: that's when he said it.

FAT MAN: Said what?

QUIET MAN: That he had a lift. That it's been out of order for months.

FAT MAN: Some hotel, I must say . . .

QUIET MAN: He is trying to get it fixed. It isn't easy. He has been recommended to get in touch with a man in Hornsey.

FAT MAN: What man?

QUIET MAN: A *lift* man I suppose. He didn't say. He just said that he must remember to get in touch with him.

FAT MAN: About what?

QUIET MAN: Well . . . the *lift*.

FAT MAN: What else did he say?

QUIET MAN: What?

FAT MAN: Did he say anything else?

QUIET MAN: About what?

FAT MAN: About anything!

QUIET MAN: Anything?

FAT MAN: Oh . . . forget it.

QUIET MAN [*pausing*]: A pity it isn't working now. He could have been up and down in no time. As it is, it will probably take him some time to make the journey . . . down . . . and up. Yes. Quite some time I should say. Unless . . . unless he *runs*. [*Pause*]. He may run.

FAT MAN: It's outrageous!

QUIET MAN: Running?

FAT MAN: The way this hotel is run. I've never seen anything like it!

QUIET MAN: *Seen* did you say? That's funny.

FAT MAN: No light! No lift! No boilers! What does he take me for!

QUIET MAN: And me.

FAT MAN: I don't know about you. . . . [*Quietly.*] What did you say your name was? [*Pause, then continuing.*] I don't know about you, but when *I* stay in an hotel I expect service. I pay good money and I expect good service.

QUIET MAN: That's reasonable. You pay good money and you expect good service. Fair enough. But you can't hold it against him.

FAT MAN: I can. And I am! If he has the temerity to call this . . . this . . . *structure* 'an hotel' he should run it as such.

QUIET MAN: You say he doesn't.

FAT MAN: I *know* he doesn't.

QUIET MAN: I think he's coming. [*Pause.*] No.

FAT MAN: You heard something?

QUIET MAN: It was nothing.

FAT MAN: Where are you now?

QUIET MAN: Still here. You?

FAT MAN: Still here. [*Pause.*] Did you notice that the rooms have been numbered illogically? Yes. They jump from the twenties to the sixties, from the thirties to the eighties, from the tens to the nineties, from five to one thousand and five!

QUIET MAN: I didn't notice.

FAT MAN: It's a fact. No clocks either. Not one clock anywhere – did you notice?

QUIET MAN: I can't say I did.

FAT MAN: It's a fact. And something else . . . on the seventh landing up I saw dead flowers in pots.

QUIET MAN: Really?

FAT MAN: I trod on a stair! It crumbled.

QUIET MAN: No . . .

FAT MAN: All the way up whole areas of banister fell away! Everywhere there is evidence of decay! You didn't notice?

QUIET MAN: Mr Barton, I . . .

FAT MAN: Where are the other guests? Where? *Are* there other guests?

QUIET MAN: They are asleep . . . in their rooms.

FAT MAN: Yes, but are they? Can we be sure? [*Pause.*] Where are you? [*Pause, then in terror.*] *Where!*

QUIET MAN: I am here, Mr Barton.

FAT MAN: Oh . . . I thought you'd left me.

QUIET MAN: Now why would I do a thing like that?

FAT MAN: You might have.

QUIET MAN: I wouldn't do a thing like that. Not to you, Mr Barton. I *like* you.

FAT MAN: It's not that I care . . . I don't care . . . don't think I care . . .

QUIET MAN: [*pausing*] To think that we are so high up from the ground. [*Pause.*] We must be in the clouds.

FAT MAN: Yes. We must be.

[*Sound of ascending footsteps. Faint, getting louder.*]

QUIET MAN: That's him this time.

FAT MAN [*to himself as a prayer*]: Hurry . . . hurry . . .

QUIET MAN: I can see the lamp!

FAT MAN: Keep away from those banisters!

QUIET MAN: There he is. Down there. I can see him. It's Mr Binks. He's running up the stairs. He must have found the key. He's coming up with it.

FAT MAN: Hurry . . . hurry . . .

QUIET MAN: Up he comes, up he comes . . .

FAT MAN: Hurry . . . hurry . . .

QUIET MAN: Up he comes, up he comes . . .

FAT MAN: Hurry . . . hurry . . .

QUIET MAN: Up . . . up . . . up . . . up . . . up . . . up . . . up . . .

[*A balanced rhythm is established: the plaintive 'hurry . . . hurry', the popping 'up . . . up . . . up' and the* LANDLORD'S *steady trot. Peak. Cut dead. Silence.*]

LANDLORD: What do you think of it?

[*They are in the room.*]

QUIET MAN: It is a charming little room.

LANDLORD: It is rather nice, isn't it?

QUIET MAN: Charming. Quite charming.

LANDLORD: Yes it is. It is.

QUIET MAN: It is a *square* room, isn't it?

LANDLORD: A *square* room. That's it.

QUIET MAN: Room Number 3 . . . 2 . . . 8 . . . 1 . . . is a charming square.

LANDLORD: Precisely. Absolutely.

QUIET MAN: A charming square in the clouds.

LANDLORD: Right up in the jolly old clouds – and soundproof into the bargain.

QUIET MAN: An altogether delightful touch!

LANDLORD: You think so?

QUIET MAN: Indeed I do.

LANDLORD [*a modest laugh*]: Yes . . . yes you could scream your head off in here and nobody would hear you. Shall I prove it?

QUIET MAN: Please do.

FAT MAN: No!

LANDLORD: It would only take a sec.

QUIET MAN: Go on, Mr Barton. Let him.

FAT MAN: We've wasted enough time as it is.

LANDLORD: It would only take a sec.

QUIET MAN: What's a sec. Mr Barton?

LANDLORD: You could spare a sec., Mr Barton.

QUIET MAN: One sec. Mr Barton. Just one.

LANDLORD: Just one. That's all.

FAT MAN [*pausing*]: It won't take any longer?

LANDLORD: No longer.

FAT MAN [*sighs*]: Very well.

LANDLORD: Good for you.

QUIET MAN: What do we do?

LANDLORD: You come with me.

FAT MAN: What!

LANDLORD: Only for a sec.

FAT MAN: What about me?

LANDLORD: You stay here. In the room.

FAT MAN: On my own?

LANDLORD [*to the* QUIET MAN]: And you come with me.

QUIET MAN: Right.

    [*They move away.*]

FAT MAN: Where are you taking him?

LANDLORD: Just outside the door. No farther than the door. [*Pause.*] Come on.

FAT MAN: You won't go away . . .

LANDLORD: No farther than the door, Mr Barton.

QUIET MAN: Don't worry, Mr Barton.

    [*Pause.*]

LANDLORD: Let's get started then.

FAT MAN: What do I have to do?

LANDLORD: Stay here. In the room. Wait for the signal.

FAT MAN: Signal?

LANDLORD [*thumps on the door three times*]: Got it?

FAT MAN: What do I do then?

    [*Pause.*]

LANDLORD [*grinning*]: Scream.

    [*Pause. Then the sound of the men departing.*]

FAT MAN [*in terror*]: The lamp!

    [*A door slams. Silence. He begins to pant again.*] Hurry . . . Hurry . . .
    [*He pants faster. He is terrified and utters sounds of terror. He moves and
    falls over his cases. He rises and falls again. He falls again and again in the
    darkness and cries 'My knee, my knee . . .'. He lies crying and panting on
    the floor. Sudden silence. Three slow thumps on the door. He screams
    hideously. Silence. The door opens. The* LANDLORD *and the* QUIET
    MAN *enter. Pause.*]

LANDLORD: You didn't scream.

FAT MAN: I did.

QUIET MAN: Incredible!

    [*Pause.*]

LANDLORD: Well then. Once again I'm sorry I couldn't find two
  singles for you but, as I explained, we are completely booked up,
  yes, booked up completely.

QUIET MAN: Think nothing of it, Mr Binks. I'm sure that Mr Barton
  and I will be very very comfortable in here.

LANDLORD: I hope so, sir. I hope so. [*Pausing.*] Oh, there's just one
  final thing.

QUIET MAN: And that is?

LANDLORD: The geography of the room, sir.

QUIET MAN: Oh that . . .

LANDLORD: It's a simple enough layout really, as layouts go . . .
  This . . . is The Chair. Four legs. Seat. Back. *Etcetera.* This . . . is
  The Bed. Head-board. Foot-board. Linen. *Etcetera.* This . . . is The
  Wardrobe.

QUIET MAN [*opening it. Head inside. Slight echo*]: It's like a little room.

LANDLORD: There are racks in it, drawers and racks, plenty of racks. And coat-hangers. Plenty of those. As many coat-hangers as racks, really. And a thin . . . wire . . . rail . . . for ties. You know. *Ties.* For anything really. But mainly for ties. It's a tie rack, see. A *tie rack.*

QUIET MAN: Everything seems to be here.

LANDLORD: That's the bathroom.

QUIET MAN: Through here? [*He opens door and enters.*]

LANDLORD: All right, sir?

QUIET MAN: Everything seems to be here . . .

LANDLORD: . . . except a lavatory, sir. There's no lavatory. There's a communal lavatory on the landing. The last door. You go out of here. Turn right. Go straight down the corridor. And it's the last door. You'll see it. It's marked. It's marked . . . 'Lavatory'. You'll see it.

QUIET MAN [*in bathroom*]: This is the sink then?

LANDLORD: Hot water left tap. Cold water right. And this . . . is the main light-switch. But as we've had a fuse blown you can forget that. That's a Table there. By The Bed.

QUIET MAN [*coming out of the bathroom*]: This?

LANDLORD: Yes. That's The Table. By The Bed. A Bed-Table. There are two of them. You can put things on those. Anything you like. Well now . . . oh yes . . . You'll find The Regulations on that wall there. You might like to glance at them. To see what's what. [*Pause.*] Well then. That's all I think. Any questions?

QUIET MAN: Where is North?

LANDLORD: Sorry, sir?

QUIET MAN: North. Where is North?

LANDLORD: North?

QUIET MAN: I'd like to know which way is North? Do you know? South would do.

LANDLORD [*confused pause.*] That's The Bathroom . . . in there. . . . Those are The Regulations . . . up there. . . . [*Pause.*] I'd better be going. Things to do. [*He moves away.*]

QUIET MAN: Thank you for all you have done.

LANDLORD: It's been a pleasure, sir. [*He stops. Pause.*] Should you require anything in the night – you never know, you might – there's a Bell, a Nightbell on the wall above the bed. I don't suppose you'll need to use it. There again . . . you never know, though, do you? [*He opens the door.*]

[*Pause. The door closes. Pause.*]

FAT MAN: Where has he gone?

QUIET MAN: *Away* . . .

FAT MAN: Why?

QUIET MAN: Things to do.

FAT MAN: What things?

QUIET MAN: Things . . . generally. You know. General things.

FAT MAN: He has taken the lamp.

QUIET MAN: That's right.

FAT MAN: This darkness . . .

QUIET MAN: Shall I strike a match? [*Pause.*] I'll strike a match. [*He does so.*] There. Is that better?

FAT MAN: This hovel! This pigsty!

QUIET MAN: I think it is a charming room.

FAT MAN [*sniffs*]: What is the smell in here?
    [*Pause.*]

QUIET MAN: Ouch!

FAT MAN: Where are you!

QUIET MAN: Here.

FAT MAN: Where!

QUIET MAN: Here. The match went out. It burned my fingers. I had to drop it.

FAT MAN: Light another! Quickly!

QUIET MAN [*lights a match, pause*]: Something wrong, Mr Barton?

FAT MAN: There's no window in here.

QUIET MAN: Why, so there isn't.

FAT MAN: There must be a window in here.

QUIET MAN: Doesn't seem to be.

FAT MAN: There must be.

QUIET MAN: Ouch!

FAT MAN: Light!
    [*Another match is struck. Pause.*]
    [*Woebegone.*] There isn't.

QUIET MAN: Don't worry. It will be all right.

FAT MAN: It's the thought of being trapped in a windowless room . . .

QUIET MAN: Try not to think about it.

FAT MAN: I can't help myself.

QUIET MAN: Try.

FAT MAN: It's no use. I can't help it.

QUIET MAN: Then we must try to take your mind off it, mustn't we? Which way is North do you think . . . That way? That way? That way? That way? [*Pause.*] Which way? [*Pause.*] And Hornsey. Which way is Hornsey do you think . . . That way? That way? That way? That way? [*Pause.*] Which way? [*Pause.*] Feeling better now?

FAT MAN [*groans*].

QUIET MAN: Ouch!

FAT MAN: Light! Light!

    [QUIET MAN *strikes another match. Pause.*]

FAT MAN: It's burning down again.

QUIET MAN: Why, so it is.

FAT MAN: Light another one.

QUIET MAN: Would you like me to?

FAT MAN: Please . . .

QUIET MAN: Supposing I were to say that this was my last.

FAT MAN: Is it?

QUIET MAN: My question first, Mr Barton.

FAT MAN: I don't know.

QUIET MAN: What?

FAT MAN: I don't know.

QUIET MAN: What?

FAT MAN: I don't know, I don't know!

QUIET MAN: What?

FAT MAN: The match!

    [*Pause.*]

QUIET MAN: It is out.

FAT MAN: Light another.

QUIET MAN: Why?

FAT MAN: Please . . .

QUIET MAN: Mr Barton. You must pull yourself together. Surely you don't expect me to stand here striking matches for you all through the night.

FAT MAN: One more.

QUIET MAN: Then another, then another . . .

FAT MAN: Just one.

QUIET MAN: There aren't many left.

FAT MAN: How many are left?

QUIET MAN [*counts them*]: Three.

FAT MAN: Use one of them now.

QUIET MAN: That would leave us with two.

FAT MAN: While it is burning I will jump into bed and go to sleep. Please . . .

QUIET MAN: Supposing you wake up?

FAT MAN: You could strike another.

QUIET MAN: And if you woke again?

FAT MAN: The last.

QUIET MAN: And if you woke again? [*Pause.*] You do see what I'm getting at, Mr Barton. To burn matches now would be wasteful, wanton and wasteful. Better to save them. Much much better to save them. Just in case.

FAT MAN: In case what?

QUIET MAN: Just in case.

FAT MAN: Give them to me.

QUIET MAN: Why?

FAT MAN: I want them.

QUIET MAN: Mr Barton, please . . .

FAT MAN [*lunges towards him and trips over the cases. He falls groaning 'My knee . . .'*].

QUIET MAN: Now you have done it.

FAT MAN: Done what?

QUIET MAN: Made me drop the matches. All three of them. That was a silly thing to do.

FAT MAN: Where are they?

QUIET MAN: On the floor. Somewhere.

FAT MAN: We must find them, we must look for them.

QUIET MAN: You look for them.

FAT MAN: Help me . . .

QUIET MAN: Very well. [*He joins the* FAT MAN *on the floor.*]

FAT MAN: Where are you?

QUIET MAN: Over here.

FAT MAN: Where?

QUIET MAN: Here.

FAT MAN: Which way?

QUIET MAN: This way.

FAT MAN: I can't see.

QUIET MAN: Walk in the direction of my voice.

FAT MAN [*moving slowly*]: I am walking.

QUIET MAN: You are walking away from me.

FAT MAN: Help me.

QUIET MAN: I can't see you.

FAT MAN: Reach out towards me.

QUIET MAN: I don't know where you are.

FAT MAN: Walk in the direction of my voice.

QUIET MAN [*moving slowly*]: I am walking.

FAT MAN: You are walking away from me!

QUIET MAN: Help me!

FAT MAN: How can I?

QUIET MAN: Where are you?

FAT MAN: Here! Here!

QUIET MAN: You're over by the door.

FAT MAN: Am I?

QUIET MAN: Reach out and see. [*Pause.*] Are you?

FAT MAN: I can feel the handle.

QUIET MAN: Turn it. Open the door.

[*The* FAT MAN *does so. He moves through the door. Pause.*]

QUIET MAN: Well?

FAT MAN [*His voice echoing plaintively*]: I'm in the *bathroom*!

QUIET MAN: Perhaps I am at the door. [*Pause. He reaches out. He touches the handle.*] I am!

FAT MAN: Open it! Open it!

[*Pause.*]

QUIET MAN [*opens the door. Pause*]: It is open.

FAT MAN [*approaching*]: Where . . . where . . . ?

QUIET MAN: Wait.

[*The* FAT MAN *stops.*]

QUIET MAN: Listen.

[*Sound of someone groping their way along the corridor – slow, menacing footsteps like those of a man who is blind. They get louder. They reach the door. They stop. Pause. A man calls quietly into the room.*]

MILITARY MAN: Anyone home?

QUIET MAN: Who is that?

MILITARY MAN: Oh. Excuse me. Is this Room Number 3281?

QUIET MAN: It is.

MILITARY MAN [*relieved*]: Thank heavens for that. Lost my bearings on the way up, what with the fuse and everything.

Had visions of spending the night on the stairs. [*Pause.*] Mind if I come in?

QUIET MAN: Please do.

MILITARY MAN [*enters. Pause*]: Suppose I ought to apologize for barging in on you like this but it's not entirely my fault.

QUIET MAN: Oh?

MILITARY MAN: No. I was sent up here.

QUIET MAN: By Mr Binks?

MILITARY MAN: Short stocky fellow. Five foot six I would say. With a moustache. He directed me here. Binks did you say his name was?

QUIET MAN: Mr Binks.

MILITARY MAN: He said the room was occupied. Asked if I minded sharing it. I said no, I don't mind sharing it, so long as the person I'm sharing it with doesn't mind. It's only for one night. Just the one. I don't mind sharing just for a night.

QUIET MAN: Have you a light on you?

MILITARY MAN: Sorry friend. Don't smoke. [*Pause.*] Pity about the fuse.

QUIET MAN: I don't mind the dark.

MILITARY MAN: Not so bad if you know where you are. Tricky in a strange hotel though. Did Binks explain why the fuse had blown?

QUIET MAN: He may have done. I can't remember.

MILITARY MAN: That's the trouble with this sort of circuit: one light goes they all go. Every last one of them. That what he told you? Still. We've got the candle. Let's be thankful for that.

QUIET MAN: The candle?

MILITARY MAN: Didn't he tell you?

QUIET MAN: What about?

MILITARY MAN: About the candle?

QUIET MAN: He said nothing about a candle.

MILITARY MAN: Funny. [*Pause.*] Know anything about the layout in here?

QUIET MAN: The geography of the room?

MILITARY MAN: The layout. Where everything is. The general set-up here.

QUIET MAN [*distant*]: The room is a charming square. In the clouds.

MILITARY MAN: What? [*Pause.*] Know where the bed is, friend?

QUIET MAN: Facing the door.

MILITARY MAN: Straight across, right?

QUIET MAN: Right.

MILITARY MAN: Right. [*He moves.*]

QUIET MAN: Mind the cases!

　　[*The* MILITARY MAN *stops dead.*]

　There are some cases . . . on the floor . . . I don't know where exactly . . . three of them . . . somewhere. Be very very careful.

MILITARY MAN: I'll take it steady. [*Moves. Stops.*] Here we are.

QUIET MAN: Found it?

MILITARY MAN: I've found the bed. Which side is the table?

QUIET MAN: You'll come to it.

MILITARY MAN [*Moves. Stops*]: I've got it . . . And I think I've got the candle . . . Yes. Panic over.

　　[*General relief.*]

　Do you have a match?

QUIET MAN: I have three matches.

MILITARY MAN: Could you light one and bring it over?

QUIET MAN: I'm afraid I can't do that.

MILITARY MAN: Oh?

QUIET MAN: No. No, I can't do that.

MILITARY MAN: Why?

QUIET MAN: Because I do not have three matches. I *had* three matches. But I do not have them now. I had them before. But something happened. And now I no longer have them.

MILITARY MAN: Where are they?

QUIET MAN: My matches are on the floor. Somewhere. I don't know where.

MILITARY MAN: Couldn't you look for them?

QUIET MAN: I could.

MILITARY MAN: Would you?

QUIET MAN: Would you like me to?

MILITARY MAN: Well . . . without matches . . . no candle . . . if you see what I mean. [*Pause.*] Go on. Have another look for them. Feel around. See if you can find them.

QUIET MAN: Yes. I'll feel around for them.

MILITARY MAN: There's a good chap.

　　[*The* QUIET MAN *moves about on the floor. He stops.*]

　Any luck?

QUIET MAN: It may be a dead one.

MILITARY MAN: Let's give it a try, shall we?

QUIET MAN: All right.

MILITARY MAN: Hand it over then.

QUIET MAN: Don't you want me to give it a try?

MILITARY MAN: If you like. I don't mind.

QUIET MAN [*pausing*]: No. No, you try it. I would rather you tried it.

MILITARY MAN: Let's have it then.

QUIET MAN: Where are you?

MILITARY MAN: By the bed-table.

QUIET MAN: I can't see you.

MILITARY MAN: Walk towards my voice.

QUIET MAN: Yes. I'll walk towards your voice. [*He moves slowly across the room. He stops. He hands over the match. Pause.*]

MILITARY MAN: Thank you. Now. [*He lights the match.*] There we are . . . it *was* a live one!

QUIET MAN: The head of the match is red. The flame is yellow.

MILITARY MAN: That's it. Now for the candle. . . . [*He lights the candle. Sound of spitting wax.*]

QUIET MAN: Two yellow flames.

MILITARY MAN: *Two* yellow flames. [*A quiet laugh.*] Now we're nice and cosy, aren't we.

QUIET MAN: Two yellow flames.

MILITARY MAN: Yes . . . two . . . nice . . . cosy . . . yellow . . . flames . . . [*He blows out the match.*] One . . . nice . . . cosy . . . yellow . . . [*He sees the* FAT MAN. *Pause.*] . . . flame. [*Pause.*] I'm sorry . . .

QUIET MAN: Sorry?

MILITARY MAN: I didn't realize there were two of you . . .

QUIET MAN: He is my friend. His name is Mr Barton.

MILITARY MAN: How do you do, Mr Barton. [*Pause.*] I suppose I owe you an apology as well for barging in like this. But as I have already explained, it is not entirely my fault. No doubt you heard me mention that I was directed here? [*Pause.*] By Mr Binks? [*Pause.*] Strange, is it not, that such an out-of-the-way hotel as this should be fully booked up . . . especially at this time of year. This will teach me to book well in advance the next time . . . if there is a next time. Personally I don't think I will be passing this way again. [*Then turning to the* QUIET MAN *and whispering.*] It's none of my business but why is he sitting on the floor?

QUIET MAN: Mr Barton, I regret to say, isn't feeling very well at the moment.

FAT MAN [*explodes to life*]: *Lies! Lies! Lies!* I'm as sound as a bell in wind and limb.

QUIET MAN: My mistake . . . [*He rises from the floor.*]

FAT MAN: The only mistake is my presence here in this room. I've had just about enough. [*He marches towards the bell.*]

MILITARY MAN: I wouldn't ring that bell if I were you.

FAT MAN [*pausing*]: Oh?

MILITARY MAN: It doesn't work, Mr Barton.

FAT MAN: What . . .

MILITARY MAN: Surely the Binks fellow told you that. He must have done. Surely he told you the bell was out of order.

FAT MAN: No . . .

MILITARY MAN: What's the matter with the man? Has he no sense of responsibility?

QUIET MAN: He is just . . . a man.

[*Pause.*]

MILITARY MAN [*looking around*]: My. This is a cosy quarter. Is there a bathroom?

QUIET MAN: Through there.

MILITARY MAN: Keep my place. I won't be long. [*He opens the door of the bathroom. He goes into the bathroom. He closes the door. Pause.*]

QUIET MAN: Pleasant man. Don't you agree?

FAT MAN: I don't care.

QUIET MAN: You are past caring.

FAT MAN: I am.

QUIET MAN: Nothing matters any more.

FAT MAN: My comfort matters.

QUIET MAN: That sounds selfish.

FAT MAN: Can I help it if I am a selfish man? Outside Forces make me selfish, the same way they make a man lustful, greedy, cruel. He is none of these things to begin with. He is made this way by Outside Forces.

QUIET MAN: Outside Forces?

FAT MAN: People. Like him in there. Like Mr Binks.

QUIET MAN: Like me?

FAT MAN: I don't know about you. Perhaps like me you are also a victim.

QUIET MAN: I have never considered myself a victim.

FAT MAN: It doesn't matter what you consider yourself. Other people make you what you are – Outside Forces! It is the Outside Forces that make you what you are . . . [*Yawns.*] I am consumed with fatigue. I think I will go to bed. [*He moves to the bed.*]

QUIET MAN: I suggest that as you are the largest amongst us you had better take the centre of the bed. By doing so you will be in no danger of falling out.

    [*Long pause.*]

FAT MAN: What did you say?

QUIET MAN: I said that I suggest that as you are the largest amongst us you had better take the centre of the bed because by doing so you will be in no danger of falling out.

    [*Long pause.*]

FAT MAN: Are you suggesting . . . that I share the bed with you two!

QUIET MAN: Well . . . there is the floor, I suppose.

FAT MAN: Now look here, young man. I've been driven far enough tonight – right to the extremity of my wits. One more push and I will not be responsible for the consequences.

QUIET MAN: But Mr Barton . . .

FAT MAN: Mr Barton nothing!

QUIET MAN: But Mr Barton . . . don't for one minute think I do not appreciate the state of mind – the terrible state of mind you are in – I do, I do, believe me. But there are certain facts we must face.

FAT MAN: There is but one fact: I am tired!

QUIET MAN: So am I. So is he. We all are.

FAT MAN: I don't care about you two!

QUIET MAN: I do. He does. Face facts, Mr Barton. There are three tired men and one bed. There is – there can be but one solution.

FAT MAN: That *I* have the bed!

QUIET MAN: That we *share* the bed.

FAT MAN: I refuse to share anything!

QUIET MAN: It may be a squeeze, but we'll manage.

FAT MAN: I refuse to share!

QUIET MAN: It will hold us all.

FAT MAN: *I refuse!*

    [*The bathroom door opens. The* MILITARY MAN *re-enters.*]

MILITARY MAN: Somebody refusing something?

FAT MAN: You keep out of this!

MILITARY MAN: Sounds like a revolt.

FAT MAN: Yes! I am revolting!

MILITARY MAN: You don't look too bad to me.

FAT MAN: How dare you . . .

QUIET MAN: Mr Barton . . .

FAT MAN: Let go of me!

MILITARY MAN: What's going on?

QUIET MAN: The sleeping arrangements.

MILITARY MAN: What about them?

QUIET MAN: There's only one bed.

MILITARY MAN: So?

QUIET MAN: There are three of us.

   [*Pause.*]

MILITARY MAN: Where's the complication? [*Pause.*] Oh . . .

FAT MAN: If you think that I am going to share that tiny bed with
   you two you had better think again. Why, the idea is outrageous –
   obscene!

MILITARY MAN: Come come, Mr Barton . . .

FAT MAN: Take your filthy hand off me!

MILITARY MAN: My dear sir, it is the hand of peace I offer.

FAT MAN [*thrown*]: Of what?

MILITARY MAN: Of peace. Of friendship. Of understanding. I
   understand your feelings.

FAT MAN: You do?

MILITARY MAN: Of course I do. And you have every right to protest against sharing a bed with two strange men. What normal,
   self-respecting Englishman wouldn't?

FAT MAN: You see my point then.

MILITARY MAN: As clearly as you stand before me. [*Pause.*] I might
   add that it is utterly refreshing to meet a man with an outlook on
   life as moral and as pure and as decent as yours, Mr Barton.

   [*Pause.*]

FAT MAN: Thank you. Thank you very much. But how does this
   affect the sleeping arrangements?

MILITARY MAN: Enormously!

FAT MAN: How . . . exactly?

MILITARY MAN [*turning*]: Friend!

QUIET MAN: You called?

MILITARY MAN: Friend . . . would you object to dossing down on the floor?

QUIET MAN: Why no. Why should I?

MILITARY MAN: Then the problem is solved.

FAT MAN: And you? Where will you sleep?

MILITARY MAN: On the floor.

FAT MAN: And the bed?

MILITARY MAN: Yours. All yours! [*Pause.*] Well now. We had better look to it, friend, and get organized. Good job it's only for the one night, eh? [*He laughs. The* QUIET MAN *laughs with him.*]

[*Fade. Pause. The three men are now lying in their respective positions: the* FAT MAN *in the bed, the others on the floor on either side of him. They all lie quietly. Pause.*]

MILITARY MAN: Quite a neat little pattern, isn't it . . . the way in which we are lying . . . the general disposition of bodies.

QUIET MAN: Mr Barton is in the bed. We are on the floor . . . on either side of him. It is a very neat pattern indeed.

MILITARY MAN: Much much better than scattering ourselves higgledy-piggledy all round the room. Why, supposing one of us were to get up in the night: it would be *chaos* in here, absolute *chaos*! People falling over one another. Bruising themselves. Ha! No. This way is much better.

QUIET MAN: It is. I much prefer this pattern best.

MILITARY MAN: Oh, yes. [*Pause.*] You see, you've got to have *Order*. Know what I mean? *Order* with a capital 'O'. Without *Order* everything goes to pieces – and when I say everything, I mean *Everything*. With a capital 'E'. You can apply that to anything. Order there must be, in anything and everything. Yes. And we've got it in this room tonight. Oh yes. I know we have. Of that I'm sure. If we've got nothing else, we've got that.

QUIET MAN: We have Order. We have Order in the clouds.

[*Pause.*]

MILITARY MAN: All right up top, Mr Barton?

FAT MAN: Yes. I'm all right.

MILITARY MAN: No complaints?

FAT MAN: None. None whatever. Everything is fine.

MILITARY MAN: Jolly dee. [*He settles down. Pause.*]

QUIET MAN:

We are a triangle. A triangle of men.

We are three bodies sleeping together. And alone.

We are a neat little pattern.

We are a Trinity.

We are the neatest pattern of all.

[*Pause.*]

MILITARY MAN [*sleepily*]: Are you comfortable, friend?

QUIET MAN: I am.

[*Pause.*]

MILITARY MAN: Then I suppose it's time for lights out. Mr Barton?

FAT MAN: Yes?

MILITARY MAN: Blow the candle out, there's a good chap.

FAT MAN: Must I?

MILITARY MAN: We can't sleep with it on, can we?

FAT MAN: Can't we?

MILITARY MAN: Suit yourself, Mr Barton. If you'd rather let it burn for a bit it's all right by me.

FAT MAN: If you don't mind . . .

MILITARY MAN: I'm easy. And I'm sure our friend is.

QUIET MAN: Yes, I'm easy.

MILITARY MAN: Blow it out when you're ready. It's all right by us.

FAT MAN: Thank you.

MILITARY MAN: Don't thank us, Mr Barton. Thank the Outside Forces that made us tolerant men. [*Yawns.*] Good night.

QUIET MAN [*distantly*]: Good night, Mr Barton.

[*They begin to fall asleep.*]

FAT MAN: Oh before you go to sleep there was something I wanted to say. It is rather in the nature of an apology . . . no, no, it is not *in the nature* of an apology – it *is* an apology, purely and simply. I . . . I . . . It's like this . . . That's to say . . . I mean . . . I mean . . .

[*The others, breathing deeply, are asleep. The* FAT MAN *sighs.*]

[*Bitterly.*] Outside Forces. They are at it again. [*He settles down. We hear the sound of three men breathing deeply. Slow fade. Silence.*]

[*Fade up the sound of two men breathing deeply. Suddenly, from somewhere deeper in the hotel, there comes the sound of a tremendous crash. The two men wake and listen, holding their breath. The crash builds as though whole portions of the building are collapsing. There is the sound of creaking timber, showering plaster, and splintering glass. It reverberates, echoes, and fades into silence. Long pause.*]

MILITARY MAN: What in Hell's name was that!

QUIET MAN: It was a *crash* . . .

MILITARY MAN: Sounded like something collapsing.

QUIET MAN: I *heard* it . . .

MILITARY MAN: What could it have been?

QUIET MAN: It came from *inside* . . .

MILITARY MAN: Funny.
  [*Pause.*]

QUIET MAN: Mr Barton all right?

MILITARY MAN: Don't know. [*Calling.*] Mr Barton? You all right?
  [*Pause.*] Mr Barton! [*Pause.*] He couldn't have slept through that
  racket.

QUIET MAN: He was very tired.

MILITARY MAN: All the same . . . [*Louder*]. Mr *Barton*! Mr *Barton*!

QUIET MAN: Shake him. Gently.

MILITARY MAN [*moving*]: It's so damned dark in here.

QUIET MAN: Shall I relight the candle?

MILITARY MAN: It's all right. I'll reach up, and feel. [*He feels the
  bed.*]

QUIET MAN: Well?

MILITARY MAN: Funny.

QUIET MAN: What?

MILITARY MAN: He isn't here.

QUIET MAN: He must be.

MILITARY MAN: The bed is empty.

QUIET MAN: It can't be.

MILITARY MAN: Feel for yourself.
  [*The* QUIET MAN *feels the bed. Pause.*]

QUIET MAN: The bed is empty. Where could he have gone?

MILITARY MAN: Ssh!

QUIET MAN: What?

MILITARY MAN: Over by the bathroom . . .

QUIET MAN: What?

MILITARY MAN: Someone breathing . . .

QUIET MAN: Do you think it's him?

MILITARY MAN [*calling quietly*]: Mr Barton. Is that you?
  [*Pause.*]

QUIET MAN: Did he answer?

MILITARY MAN: No . . .

QUIET MAN: Perhaps he's hurt. [*Calls quietly.*] Mr Barton. Are you hurt?

MILITARY MAN: Are you hurt? [*Pause.*] What's the matter with him?

QUIET MAN: Perhaps he's fainted. The crash may have frightened him.

MILITARY MAN: Possible. [*Pause.*] We'd better get up and see. [*Rising.*] Coming? [*He moves away.*]

QUIET MAN [*also moving*]: I'm right behind you . . .
    [*They move blindly round the room. Pause.*]

MILITARY MAN: Here we are.

QUIET MAN: Where are you?

MILITARY MAN: Over here. By the bathroom. Where are you?

QUIET MAN: By the other door.

MILITARY MAN: What are you doing there?

QUIET MAN: Following you.

MILITARY MAN: I'm over here.

QUIET MAN: You can't be. I was following.

MILITARY MAN: You couldn't have been.

QUIET MAN: I was following somebody.

MILITARY MAN: You couldn't have been following me. I'm over here.

QUIET MAN: Then who was I following?

MILITARY MAN: Never mind. Just get over here and give me a hand.

QUIET MAN: Coming . . . coming . . . [*He moves away.*]

MILITARY MAN: Now then, Mr Barton. What are you doing out of bed? And why no answer when we called? You had us worried.

QUIET MAN [*approaching*]: Is he saying anything?

MILITARY MAN: Nothing.

QUIET MAN: He must have fainted.

MILITARY MAN: Impossible.

QUIET MAN: Why?

MILITARY MAN: He's standing up. [*Pause.*] Better light the candle, friend.

QUIET MAN: Right. [*He gropes his way to the bed-table, strikes a match and lights the candle. Pause.*]

MILITARY MAN: Well. Well. Well.

QUIET MAN: Mr Binks!

LANDLORD: Hello, sir.

[*Pause.*]

MILITARY MAN: And what, may we ask, are *you* doing here?

LANDLORD: There's been a complication, sir.

MILITARY MAN: What kind of a complication?

LANDLORD: A collapse, sir.

MILITARY MAN: Whereabouts?

LANDLORD: In the West Wing, sir.

MILITARY MAN: The West Wing?

LANDLORD: The West Wing. Yes, sir.

MILITARY MAN: Serious?

LANDLORD: Very.

MILITARY MAN: Casualties?

LANDLORD: Not sure, sir.

MILITARY MAN: Not *sure*!

LANDLORD: Not yet, sir. You see, most of the rooms were empty.

MILITARY MAN: You told me the hotel was full.

LANDLORD: Apart from the West Wing it was.

[*Pause.*]

MILITARY MAN: There's something wrong . . . with the West Wing?

LANDLORD: It just worked out that way.

MILITARY MAN: There's something *wrong* . . . with the West Wing?

LANDLORD: Foundation trouble.

MILITARY MAN: What kind?

LANDLORD: General . . . General.

QUIET MAN [*remembering*]: There was a *crash* . . .

LANDLORD: That's right, sir.

QUIET MAN: A loud, *echoing* crash . . .

LANDLORD: Echoing. Yes . . .

MILITARY MAN: The West Wing . . . is down?

LANDLORD: Practically.

MILITARY MAN: Some is left?

LANDLORD: Bits.

MILITARY MAN: What bits?

LANDLORD: One room.

MILITARY MAN: Yes?

LANDLORD: One landing.

MILITARY MAN: And under them?

LANDLORD: Thin air.

MILITARY MAN: And over them?

LANDLORD: Stars.

QUIET MAN: And over them . . . *stars* . . .
   [*Pause.*]

MILITARY MAN [*closer*]: Have you seen . . . Mr Barton?

LANDLORD: I haven't.

MILITARY MAN: Are you sure?

LANDLORD: Positive. Is he missing?

MILITARY MAN: You know he is. Don't blush.

LANDLORD: Who's blushing?

MILITARY MAN: You.

LANDLORD: I'm hot. I've been running about. Yes. I've been running about.

MILITARY MAN: You have been standing right here. In this room. You heard us calling Mr Barton.

LANDLORD: You're right. Yes. I remember now. I did. I heard you calling for him, I distinctly remember hearing.
   [*Pause.*]

MILITARY MAN: What were you doing in our room, Mr Binks?

LANDLORD: I came to tell you . . .

MILITARY MAN: Tell us?

LANDLORD: To warn you, to warn you . . .

MILITARY MAN: Warn us?

LANDLORD: About the West Wing collapsing.

MILITARY MAN: You were here when it collapsed.

LANDLORD: That's right. I was here.

MILITARY MAN: Then you were here . . . *before* it collapsed.

LANDLORD: In a manner of speaking. Yes.

MILITARY MAN: Yes or no, Mr Binks!

LANDLORD: Yes! Yes!

MILITARY MAN: Ready to warn us if it *did* collapse.

LANDLORD: I knew it was going to collapse.

MILITARY MAN: You knew?

LANDLORD: I was expecting it. I've been expecting it to collapse for donkey's years. I knew about the foundation trouble, see.

MILITARY MAN: So you let us go to bed. Then returned when we were sleeping.

LANDLORD: Something like that. Yes.

MILITARY MAN: You stood by us. Ready to give the alarm.

LANDLORD: Yes.

MILITARY MAN: You came into our room for no other reason.

LANDLORD: Other than to warn you, no.

MILITARY MAN: For no other reason?

LANDLORD: None.

MILITARY MAN: No other reason at all?

LANDLORD: None. None at all.

[Pause.]

MILITARY MAN [closer still]: There's nothing going on, is there?

LANDLORD: Going on?

MILITARY MAN: You know . . . going on.

LANDLORD: I don't know what you mean.

MILITARY MAN: Don't you?

LANDLORD: I don't . . . I don't.

[Pause.]

MILITARY MAN: We'll discuss this later. [He moves towards the door.]

LANDLORD [intercepting him]: Where are you going?

MILITARY MAN: To the remains of the West Wing. Out of my way.

LANDLORD: No.

MILITARY MAN: Coming, friend?

QUIET MAN: I am with you. [He follows.]

LANDLORD [panicking]: No . . .

MILITARY MAN: Men may be trapped, wounded. We must rescue them.

LANDLORD: You can't . . .

MILITARY MAN: It is our duty.

LANDLORD: You don't know the way . . .

MILITARY MAN: You will tell us.

LANDLORD: Oh, will I?

MILITARY MAN: Oh yes. You will tell us. [He grabs hold of the LAND-LORD. Sound of a struggle.] I'm a tolerant man, Binks, but I draw the line at cowards.

LANDLORD: Let go . . .

MILITARY MAN: Tell us . . .

LANDLORD: You're choking me . . .

MILITARY MAN: The way . . . to the West Wing . . .

LANDLORD [gasping]: You are there! . . . This is it!

[*Sound of creaking timber and plaster showering down – the room is collapsing.*]

[*In terror.*] The floor's going in!

QUIET MAN: What?

MILITARY MAN: Jump for it! Into the corridor!

[*They jump. The room collapses. Sounds as before – reverberating, echoing, and fading into silence. Pause. Fade up soft wind. Hold under. The men are now on the landing. Below them thin air. Above them stars.*]

MILITARY MAN: Well. That's that.

QUIET MAN: Our room has *gone* . . .

MILITARY MAN: That's right, friend. Our room has gone. We no longer have a quarter.

QUIET MAN: No quarter . . .

MILITARY MAN: None.

QUIET MAN: We are on the landing . . .

MILITARY MAN: Marooned. Utterly and completely.

QUIET MAN: We are marooned . . . in the *clouds* . . .

MILITARY MAN: Precisely. [*Pause.*] You've got us into quite a fix. [*Pause.*] Haven't you, Mr Binks?

LANDLORD: I . . . I . . .

MILITARY MAN: *Haven't* you?

LANDLORD: Well, yes. I suppose I have.

MILITARY MAN: My friend and I are curious to know precisely what you intend to do about it.

LANDLORD: Do?

MILITARY MAN: Do.

LANDLORD: What can I do?

MILITARY MAN: That is for you to decide. We are in your hands now.

LANDLORD: I feel so helpless . . . I didn't account for this . . . not this . . .

MILITARY MAN: Then you had better start accounting. It has *happened*. It is *real*.

LANDLORD: I don't know what to suggest. [*Pause.*] This landing might go next . . .

MILITARY MAN: That's right.

LANDLORD: We'll all go with it!

MILITARY MAN: Unless you think of something.

LANDLORD: What?

MILITARY MAN: That is for you to decide. You were responsible for getting us up here. You are responsible for getting us down. [*Pause.*] Well?
    [*Pause.*]

LANDLORD: I don't know . . . I just don't know.
    [*A moan comes out of the darkness. The* LANDLORD *gasps. Pause.*]

QUIET MAN: I heard a sound . . .

MILITARY MAN: So did I.

QUIET MAN: It was a *moaning* sound. It came from over there . . .

MILITARY MAN: Can you see what it is?

LANDLORD: If only we had the lamp!

MILITARY MAN: Can you see something now?

QUIET MAN: I do believe I can.

MILITARY MAN: What?

LANDLORD: What can he see?

MILITARY MAN: Ssh!

LANDLORD: I don't like it!

MILITARY MAN: Quiet!

LANDLORD: I'm scared!

MILITARY MAN: Hold your tongue!

LANDLORD: That *thing* over there, what is it!
    [*Pause.*]

QUIET MAN: I think . . . it is a *man* . . .

MILITARY MAN: Who?
    [*Pause.*]

QUIET MAN: It's Mr Barton . . . [*He moves away.*]

LANDLORD: Where's he going?

MILITARY MAN: To rescue Mr Barton.

LANDLORD: He mustn't! Stop him! Stop him!
    [*The* MILITARY MAN *deals him a deadly blow. The* LANDLORD *falls with a cry.*]

MILITARY MAN: Carry on, friend. Everything's under control.
    [*Fade. We hear the* FAT MAN *moaning. He sounds injured.*]

QUIET MAN [*approaching*]: Mr Barton . . .

FAT MAN [*screaming*]: Keep back!

QUIET MAN: I am your friend.

FAT MAN: Don't touch me! Go away!

QUIET MAN: I won't hurt you.

FAT MAN: Go away . . . leave me . . . there's nothing in the cases . . .

MILITARY MAN [*calling over*]: What's he saying?

QUIET MAN: Nothing in your cases, Mr Barton?

FAT MAN: Nothing . . . nothing . . . they are empty . . . all three of them . . . now leave me . . .

MILITARY MAN [*calling over*]: What's he doing?

QUIET MAN [*to himself*]: He's crying . . . His tears are on my hand.

MILITARY MAN [*calling over*]: Get him over here!

QUIET MAN: Come on, Mr Barton. Up you come. [*He helps the* FAT MAN *to his feet.*]

FAT MAN: Where are you taking me?

QUIET MAN: Don't worry. You'll be all right. There is nothing to worry about. We are only marooned. [*He moves away.*]

FAT MAN: Marooned? [*Pause.*] Wait for me . . . [*moving away*] Wait for me . . . wait for me . . .

[*Fade. Pause.*]

MILITARY MAN: We meet again, Mr Barton.

FAT MAN: Who is that?

QUIET MAN: The other man.

FAT MAN: What other man?

QUIET MAN: The other man in the room. There were three of us, remember?

FAT MAN: There were more . . .

QUIET MAN: Only the three of us, Mr Barton.

FAT MAN: There were more! [*Pause, then quietly.*] Who else is here?

QUIET MAN: Mr Binks.

FAT MAN: Where?

MILITARY MAN: Lying down, Mr Barton. He isn't very well.

FAT MAN: Who else is here?

QUIET MAN: Just the four of us.

FAT MAN: And the others?

MILITARY MAN: What others?

FAT MAN: There are *others* I tell you!

MILITARY MAN: Who?

FAT MAN: Men. Two men. They beat me!

MILITARY MAN: Beat you? When?

FAT MAN: In the night. You were sleeping. [*Pause.*] Am I dead?

MILITARY MAN: Physically no.

FAT MAN: Technically? [*Pause.*] I don't want to be. Much too much to be done. Too many mistakes to rectify. False moves to correct.

Too many apologies to make. I don't want to be dead.
[*Pause.*]

MILITARY MAN: You were saying . . . about the men.

FAT MAN: They beat me.

MILITARY MAN: When did they come?

FAT MAN: When you were sleeping.

MILITARY MAN: Did you see them?

FAT MAN: The candle was out . . . not to begin with . . . to begin with it was almost out . . . the wick floating in a pool of wax . . . a floating flame. I lay there waiting for the darkness. Then it came. As soon as it came I heard sounds . . . in the corridor . . . footsteps . . . whispering . . . laughter. It sounded like people coming. They reached the door. They stopped. I lay there. The door opened slowly. I called out to them, *who are you?* They came towards me. [*Pause.*] And then I knew.

MILITARY MAN: Knew what?

FAT MAN: What they were after.

MILITARY MAN: What were they after?

FAT MAN [*crying*]: My *cases!*

QUIET MAN: They were empty.

FAT MAN: I told them. They laughed. They thought I was joking. I protested. They beat me! I must have fainted . . . then I came round . . . I was no longer in the room.

MILITARY MAN: Where were you?

FAT MAN: In the corridor . . . bleeding like a pig in the dark! [*Crying.*] My face . . .

MILITARY MAN: And the men?
[*Pause.*]

FAT MAN: They had gone.
[*Pause.*]

QUIET MAN: It must have been *them* I followed round the room.

FAT MAN: Who were they?
[*The* LANDLORD *groans.*]

MILITARY MAN: Ask Mr Binks.

LANDLORD [*dazed*]: Where am I . . .

MILITARY MAN: On the landing.

LANDLORD: What happened . . .

MILITARY MAN: You bumped into something.

LANDLORD [*pausing*]: Mr Barton's here . . .

FAT MAN: Who *were* they?

LANDLORD: Who?

FAT MAN: The *men*!

LANDLORD: What men?

FAT MAN: The men who beat and robbed me!

LANDLORD: Who what?

FAT MAN: Who beat and *robbed* me! [*He sniffs unhappily.*]

LANDLORD: I don't know what he's talking about.

MILITARY MAN [*threatening*]: You do . . .

LANDLORD: I don't! *What* men! *What* men!

MILITARY MAN: You tell us . . .

LANDLORD: *I* don't know! [*He cries out.*]

MILITARY MAN [*gripping him*]: Out with it, traitor . . .

LANDLORD: Let go . . .

MILITARY MAN: Who were they . . .

LANDLORD: I don't know . . .

MILITARY MAN: Who . . . who . . .

    [*Pause.*]

LANDLORD [*choking*]: Mr *Green*! . . . and Mr *Brown*!

MILITARY MAN: You sent them there . . .

LANDLORD: I sent them . . .

MILITARY MAN: *Lies!* You *brought* them! *Personally!* [*He throws the*
    LANDLORD *down. The* LANDLORD *whimpers.*]

LANDLORD: I didn't want to . . . they made me . . . they *made* me . . .

MILITARY MAN: *Scum!*

    [*The* LANDLORD *gasps for air.*]

QUIET MAN: But the cases were empty!

MILITARY MAN: So what! It's a question of loyalty. Allegiance!
    We are his guests! Right left and centre he has let us down! Well
    now it's his turn to be let down.

QUIET MAN: What are you going to do with him?

MILITARY MAN: Make a man of him.

QUIET MAN: How?

MILITARY MAN: By giving him a chance to die – not neglecting
    but doing his duty. While you were out there rescuing Mr Bar-
    ton, I made a brief reconnaissance of the landing. I learned that
    there is still one feature of the West Wing *intacto*.

QUIET MAN: Which feature is that?

MILITARY MAN [*pausing*]: The lift shaft.

LANDLORD [*in anticipation*]: No . . . I won't go . . .

MILITARY MAN: I repeat: now it's your turn to be let down . . .

LANDLORD: No . . .

MILITARY MAN: The rope will hold you, Mr Binks. You will descend the shaft and sound the alert.

LANDLORD: It won't hold me!

MILITARY MAN: Then you will die a hero.

LANDLORD [*backing away*]: You can't make me . . .

MILITARY MAN [*following him*]: You have no desire to redeem yourself?

LANDLORD: I'm not going. Keep back!

MILITARY MAN: You are going to descend the shaft, Mr Binks . . .

LANDLORD: Keep back!

[*Their voices begin to fade.*]

MILITARY MAN: You are going down, Mr Binks . . .

LANDLORD: No. No. No. No . . .

[*Fade. Long pause. The sound of a long falling scream. It fades into silence. Long pause. The sound of footsteps returning. They stop. Pause.*]

LANDLORD [*panting*]: He slipped. The gates were open. I've been meaning to get them fixed for ages – could I find anyone to fix them? He leaned over to open them – it wasn't my fault they were open! Nothing was my fault . . . The boilers . . . the fuse . . . the bell . . . the lift . . . the gates . . . Outside Forces. Know what I mean? They were responsible, not me. I'm not guilty of anything, I'm . . . I'm all right. And I'll redeem myself. You wait and see if I don't.

QUIET MAN: Where are you going, Mr Binks?

LANDLORD: It's all right. I'm only going to look for the men – Mr Brown and Mr Green. Mr B. and Mr G. They'll vouchsafe for my character. [*Going.*] They'll vouchsafe for my character.

[*His footsteps fade. Soft wind. Hold under. Long pause.*]

FAT MAN: Where are you?

QUIET MAN: I am here.

FAT MAN: And the others?

QUIET MAN: They have all gone away.

FAT MAN: Will they be back?

QUIET MAN: They might be. It's hard to say.

[*Pause. The FAT MAN groans.*]

FAT MAN: My head . . .

QUIET MAN: Is it hurting you?

FAT MAN: When I move it . . .

QUIET MAN: Try not to. Stand still.

[*Pause.*]

FAT MAN: Will we ever get down from here?

QUIET MAN: You mustn't worry about that.

FAT MAN: I want to know. If we are going to be stuck here for ever
. . . there are certain things I have to do.

QUIET MAN: What things?

FAT MAN: Mistakes to rectify. False moves to correct. Apologies to
make.

QUIET MAN: You have sinned?

FAT MAN [*sighs*]: Over and over and over . . .

[*Pause.*]

QUIET MAN: You may confess your sins to me – not now. Later.
When we are settled. Meanwhile . . . let us consider ourselves in
relation to the Universe as a whole . . . determine in which direction lies the North. [*Pause.*] Once we know this, we will know
where Hornsey lies . . . [*Pause.*] And Bethlehem. [*Pause.*] We will
do this standing still, Mr Barton.

[*Pause.*]

FAT MAN: Standing still.

[*Pause.*]

QUIET MAN: Nothing terrible will happen to us. So long as we are
standing . . . still.

[*They stand still. Soft wind. Slow fade.*]

END

CARYL CHURCHILL

The Ants

The Ants was first broadcast on the B.B.C. Third
Programme on 27 November 1962 with the following cast:

GRANDFATHER	Lockwood West
JANE	Diana Olsson
STEWART	Derek Blomfield
TIM	David Palmer

Produced by Michael Bakewell

TIM: Hello, ant, what are you carrying? Is it something to eat? Is it? You're carrying something too, and you are, and you are, and you – here, don't stop. The others aren't stopping, you've got to get over to the other side of the veranda. What's the matter? Go on then. Where are you going? Along, along, into the crack. Into the crack and I can't see. They come out of it too. Here you, little one, you're smaller than the others, come on my finger, come on. Don't be frightened, don't run away. Come on, dear little . . . There's another little one going the other way. You're little, you're little, you're middle, you're big. Big and shiny. What will you do if I put a twig in the way? You get over easily, don't you? Come on, you can, too. Come on, ants. [*Laughs.*]

GRANDFATHER: Well, there's another day over. It's six o'clock again. It always seems to be six o'clock now. Every day I notice when it's six o'clock and it means another day's over.

JANE [*calls off*]: Tim!
    [*Pause.*]

GRANDFATHER: Tim, your mother's calling.

JANE [*nearer*]: What are you doing?

TIM: Nothing.

JANE [*on the veranda*]: Are you clean? Your father's going to arrive any minute, I don't want him to think I don't look after you. What's that? Ants? This house is disgusting, earwigs in the kitchen, there's something moving wherever you look. What do you do to ants, Dad?

GRANDFATHER: Do you have to do anything?

JANE: You can put petrol on them and set fire to it, can't you?

TIM: No.

JANE: Tim, go and get washed, dear.

TIM: They're my ants. You're not going to hurt them.

JANE: Wash your face and hands and comb your hair. And put on a clean shirt, and some sandals, what have you done with your sandals?

TIM: You can't kill them, they're ants.

GRANDFATHER: We won't touch them, Tim. Go and do what your mother says. Go on now.

TIM [*going off*]: Daddy won't let you kill them.

JANE [*calling after him*]: Don't forget to comb your hair. You see? He plays us off against each other, 'Daddy won't let you.' It's as if he knew.

GRANDFATHER: You can't expect him not to notice anything.

JANE: But it's as if he's saying, 'If you're not nice to me you won't get custody of me, I'll go to Daddy.'

GRANDFATHER: Won't that be up to the court?

JANE: Yes, of course it will, I'm certain to get him. They can't take a child away from its mother.

GRANDFATHER: I don't know about these things. Won't it depend on who they decide is the – what? The guilty party?

JANE: Stewart's the guilty party.

GRANDFATHER: What time is he coming?

JANE: He's late.

GRANDFATHER: You're looking very lovely. I haven't seen that dress before. Is there really any need to go so far as getting a divorce? [*Pause.*] I suppose it depends on whether Stewart thinks you're looking lovely.

JANE: It's all right for you to be sentimental, Father, it's not your life.

GRANDFATHER: I just think you might as well settle for the mediocrity you know. The best you can hope for by leaving him is misery and tragedy and you probably won't even get that, you'll just be bored again.

JANE: It's your fault I married him. You kept having him to stay, what could I do? I never saw anyone else.

GRANDFATHER: You loved him.

JANE: Oh, I don't know.

GRANDFATHER: The thing is I find it very hard to care about you. It's hard enough to care about other people anyway, but when you get old and no one cares about you it's even worse. You're not the centre of anyone's life except your own, so there's nothing to make you notice other people. And if your head aches or your feet are cold, there's nothing as important as your feet and your head and your back.

[*Sound of car arriving.*]

JANE: Tim does love me, doesn't he?

GRANDFATHER: I love you too. I think even Stewart loves you, you're a lucky girl.

JANE: Well that was his car.

GRANDFATHER: Go and meet him then.

JANE: Yes. He'll come through to the veranda, I'll stay here.

GRANDFATHER: Yes, lean on the rail, look out at the sea, ignore him. You look very nice like that.

TIM [*calling*]: Mummy, Mummy, Daddy's here.

JANE [*loudly*]: We're on the veranda, Stewart.

TIM: Come on, Daddy. Here he is, Mummy. Look, he gave me some chocolate.

JANE: Not before supper, Tim.

STEWART: Hello, Jane.

JANE: Hello, Stewart.

STEWART: Good evening, Grandpa.

GRANDFATHER: You used to call me Arthur and now you call me Grandpa. You've slipped two generations.

STEWART: You're looking very well.

GRANDFATHER: Nothing happens here. The days drop into the sea out there as they used to when you first came, plop, plop, as the sun drops into the horizon.

TIM: Daddy, look at the ants.

STEWART: Well, aren't they fine?

JANE: Is that an evening paper, Stewart? Can I see it? We never seem to get a paper here.

STEWART: Yes, of course. Here.

GRANDFATHER: Yes, you forget there's a world outside and a war on. You can't imagine a war down here, but there's always one somewhere.

JANE: They've dropped a big bomb.

GRANDFATHER: Which side?

JANE: Us.

GRANDFATHER: Dropped it on us?

JANE: No, we dropped it.

GRANDFATHER: I suppose that's just as well.

TIM: Can you watch one ant, Daddy?

STEWART: No, I lose track of them. They all look the same.

TIM: I think there's one I know. He's a bit red. His name's Bill.

JANE: Do you want to go for a walk before dinner, Stewart?

STEWART: Yes, let's do that. Coming, Tim?

JANE: I expect Tim wants to play with his ants.

TIM: Yes.

STEWART: Where shall we go then?

JANE: Down to the sea?

STEWART: In those shoes?

JANE: I'll change them.

STEWART: All right, be quick.

JANE: I don't have to go upstairs. I've some sandals in the hall, come on.

[*They go off.* GRANDFATHER *reads the paper.*]

GRANDFATHER: Ten thousand dead. Well. Typist to wed Maharajah. President's dog has puppies. Backs are in fashion. Duke jumps in fountain. My Desire at 100–1. Nothing in the paper. How's Bill?

TIM: I'm not sure where he is just at the moment. I think he's gone under the wall, he'll be back in a minute.

GRANDFATHER: Go on, you won't know him again.

TIM: I will.

GRANDFATHER: How did you meet him?

TIM: He wandered away from the others, I nearly knelt on him, so I put him back.

GRANDFATHER: What did he do then?

TIM: He ran round and round as if he wasn't sure where to go, and talked to some of the others about it, and then came down here. Look, there he is.

GRANDFATHER: Are you sure?

TIM: Yes.

GRANDFATHER: What about that one?

TIM: No, this one.

GRANDFATHER: Where?

TIM: Here – no, oh, where is he? Which one is he?

GRANDFATHER: You can't tell one from the other.

TIM: Oh –!

GRANDFATHER: How many ants are there here?

TIM: Millions.

GRANDFATHER: Ten thousand?

TIM: Yes, ten thousand. Is Daddy staying long?

GRANDFATHER: I think he's here for the weekend.

TIM: Till Monday?

GRANDFATHER: Or Sunday night.

TIM: Don't you know which?

GRANDFATHER: Does it matter?

TIM: I don't know. Can we give the ants something to eat?

GRANDFATHER: Yes, I know, give them some sugar. I'll give them a
teaspoon of sugar.

[*While he gets the sugar* TIM *leans over the rail of the veranda.*]

TIM: I can see Mummy and Daddy on the beach. They can't see me,
they're not looking. They look very small.

GRANDFATHER: Here we are.

TIM: Why doesn't Daddy come here for longer?

GRANDFATHER: He's busy at the office all week.

TIM: But he doesn't come every weekend.

GRANDFATHER: Come and see the ants eating the sugar.

TIM [*goes back to the ants*]: Are we going home with Daddy at the end
of the summer?

GRANDFATHER: Do you want to?

TIM: I like the summer.

GRANDFATHER: Look at them, they're just like people. Greedy,
greedy. They don't know what to do, they didn't allow for that,
ooh, isn't it nice. Look at them all telling each other about it,
nasty, greedy things.

They're very intelligent, ants, as intelligent as people anyway.
They've got everything organized, they all work together for their
society. Look at them, tramp, tramp, back and forth, fetching and
carrying, working for their living. Very smug they are about it,
too. If an ant meets a grasshopper in the winter he says, 'What did
you do all summer?' and the poor cold grasshopper says, 'I danced
and sang in the sun', and the horrid self-righteous ant says, 'I
worked hard so I've plenty to eat, you go to hell', and the poor
grasshopper dies of cold and hunger.

TIM: I like ants.

GRANDFATHER: They've no imagination, just like people. Have you
ever looked at a crowd of people? Run, run, run. Look at them
from the top of a tall building some time, just funny patterns of
people, or out of an aeroplane, funny little toy towns, coloured
targets, and not even people then, just black ant motorcars.

TIM: Have you been in an aeroplane?

GRANDFATHER: Yes.

TIM: Where did you go?

GRANDFATHER: I came back to England.

TIM: Where from?

GRANDFATHER: New York.

TIM: What were you doing in New York?

GRANDFATHER: I really don't know.

TIM: Was it nice in the aeroplane?

GRANDFATHER: I didn't really notice.

TIM: What's the point of being in it then?

GRANDFATHER: I was in a hurry.

TIM: Why?

GRANDFATHER: Your grandmother was dying.

TIM: In the plane?

GRANDFATHER: No, here in this house.

TIM: Why wasn't she in New York?

GRANDFATHER: She was in England.

TIM: Was it a jet?

GRANDFATHER: I don't think so.

TIM: How many engines did it have?

GRANDFATHER: I don't remember. You can't find Bill now, can you? Oh, I'm stiff. Oh. I'm an old man. I shouldn't get down on the ground like that. I should stay in my chair. Ah. [*He sits down.*]

TIM: When are Mummy and Daddy coming back?

GRANDFATHER: Supper-time.

TIM: I'm hungry. I can't see them, can you?

GRANDFATHER: I wouldn't see them even if they were there, my eyes are too old.

TIM: You aren't even looking.

GRANDFATHER: I couldn't see them if I did look.

TIM: I expect they've gone to the caves.

GRANDFATHER: So we've dropped a big bomb.

TIM: How big?

GRANDFATHER: Very big.

TIM: Did it kill a lot of people?

GRANDFATHER: Yes.

TIM: I expect it killed more people than any bomb's ever done before.

GRANDFATHER: That's good, is it?

TIM: You're meant to kill the enemy in a war.

GRANDFATHER: Yes, that's true.

TIM: Did you drop bombs out of your plane?

GRANDFATHER: No.

TIM: What did you do?

GRANDFATHER: I read magazines.

TIM: Is that when Granny died?

GRANDFATHER: Yes, she died before I got back.

TIM: I want my supper. [*He calls over the rail.*] Mum-my! Dad-dy!
  I'm hun-gry!

GRANDFATHER: They won't hear you.

TIM: Is Uncle Peter coming this weekend?

GRANDFATHER: No.

TIM: When is he coming?

GRANDFATHER: Do you like him?

TIM: He catches a lot of fish.

GRANDFATHER: Would you like him to be around all the time?

TIM: Is he coming to live with you?

GRANDFATHER: If he came to live with you.

TIM: You live all by yourself.

GRANDFATHER: Not at the moment.

TIM: Do you like it?

GRANDFATHER: I've got the ants for company.

TIM: Mummy wants to kill the ants.

GRANDFATHER: We won't kill them.

TIM: How did she say do it? With petrol?

GRANDFATHER: You pour petrol on and set light to it.

TIM: Does petrol burn?

GRANDFATHER: Yes.

TIM: But it's wet. Does water burn?

GRANDFATHER: No.

TIM: If water burned you could burn up the sea. [*Pause.*] What else
  can we do with the ants?

GRANDFATHER: Why do anything with them?

TIM: They're a bit boring just going up and down.

GRANDFATHER: They don't know about you.

TIM: They do if I give them sugar and put a twig in front of them.

GRANDFATHER: They know sugar and the twig, they don't know
  you.

TIM: I wonder where Bill is?

GRANDFATHER: They have terrible ants in foreign countries. They march in great armies, enormous ants eating their way through a jungle. They eat everything in their way.

TIM: Would they eat you if you got in their way?

GRANDFATHER: They might do.

TIM: They wouldn't eat me, I'd stamp on them.

GRANDFATHER: There'd be too many.

TIM: I'd jump and jump.

GRANDFATHER: Too many.

TIM: I'd drop things on them.

GRANDFATHER: There are too many. They make whole houses fall down. Locusts, too, great plagues of locusts stripping countries bare. Great seething masses of insects, you can't see any one of them, just masses and masses, destroying everything in their way. Think if you couldn't have any supper because the ants and locusts had eaten it all.

TIM: I wouldn't let them.

GRANDFATHER: Then try to stop them. Poor people run out with gongs and they beat and beat and beat to make a loud noise so the locusts won't come down on their crops, they run in the cornfields shouting and banging metal, but they do come down somewhere in the end.

TIM: Do ants go away if you shout at them?

GRANDFATHER: Try.

TIM [crouches down on the ground. Shouts]: Go away, ants. Go away.

GRANDFATHER: Nowadays they're scientific, they spray the locusts and kill miles and miles of them. They fly up in aeroplanes and aim poison at them.

TIM: What about ants? They don't go away when you shout.

GRANDFATHER: I don't know what they do about them.

TIM: You didn't mind me shouting, did you, ant? Come on my finger. There, where will you go on my hand? It's a long time since Daddy's been here.

GRANDFATHER: He's very busy.

TIM: Look, there's Bill. You come on my hand, too. Now he won't be lonely. What was your job?

GRANDFATHER: Oh, I worked for a company like most people.

TIM: Did you like it? [To ants.] Come on.

GRANDFATHER: No, it was a silly place. Like these ants in the city every day.

TIM: Now I've got four on my hand.

GRANDFATHER: They thought I was silly, too, so they sent me away in the end.

TIM [*to ants*]: No, not up my arm, on my hand. They sent you to New York?

GRANDFATHER: It was after that I went to New York, yes.

TIM: Were you away as long as Daddy's been away? Come on, ants, come on my hand. Come on, more of you.

GRANDFATHER: A bit longer.

TIM: Didn't you like Granny any more? [*Pause.*] Daddy doesn't like us.

GRANDFATHER: Of course he does.

TIM [*to ants*]: Not up my arm. Keep still. He doesn't live with us.

GRANDFATHER: Would you rather live with him or Mummy?

TIM: Yes, that's what they want to know. They're always going to live apart, aren't they?

GRANDFATHER: Who would you rather live with?

TIM [*suddenly, in horror of the ants*]: Oh! Oh! Go away! Oh!

GRANDFATHER: What is it?

TIM: There were too many ants.

GRANDFATHER: They won't hurt you.

TIM: I don't like it, there were too many. I started out with one or two on my hand and I could see each of them all the time and one of them was Bill, and then suddenly there were lots of ants all over my fingers and up my arm and I couldn't tell where they all were, and I tried to knock them off my arm and they wouldn't get off and I couldn't tell where they were –

GRANDFATHER: You've hurt them, you've squashed some of them.

TIM: Oh! Do something.

GRANDFATHER: Never mind.

TIM: Do something. They're all squirming.

GRANDFATHER: Stamp on them.

TIM: No.

GRANDFATHER: Stamp on them.

TIM: No. You do it.

GRANDFATHER: Like this. [*He stamps on the crushed ants, wipes his foot.*]

TIM: Ohhh.

GRANDFATHER: Don't be silly. They're just ants.

[*Pause.*]

TIM: Can't I live by myself like you?

GRANDFATHER: Not till you're older.

TIM: When I'm older I don't want to live with anyone.

GRANDFATHER: No, you remember that. You'll think you do some time, but remember what you said just now. You'll think you want to live with some girl and have lots of children and friends and jobs and live in a happy ant hill, but you don't, remember that. You want to be all by yourself and see the silly ants going up and down and give them sugar and stamp on them. Don't be fooled by love or vocation, you keep by yourself and you won't have to desert anyone later.

TIM: What do you mean?

GRANDFATHER: Desertion. Don't you know what desert is?

TIM: Like pudding dessert?

GRANDFATHER: No, like sandy desert. Desertion is me leaving your grandmother and your father leaving your mother. Desertion is when you stop loving people and see them from miles above, when you lose them and see just a lot of black ants.

TIM: I don't know what you mean.

GRANDFATHER: And you know what adultery is? Not adult grown-up, adultery?

TIM: No.

GRANDFATHER: Adultery's Uncle Peter, and if you live by yourself you won't have that either. Live by yourself by the sea, remember that. You're edging away, to the rail. Yes, you watch the sea.

TIM: I don't know what you mean.

GRANDFATHER: I mean nobody loves anyone, that's what I mean. I'm an old man and it's all too late and nobody loves anyone. Out there they're all dropping bombs, bang, bang, bang, I don't know, I only know about me, I'm an old man and I'm stiff and cold, and none of us love each other.

TIM: Mummy and Daddy are coming. I can see them coming on the beach.

GRANDFATHER: Where?

TIM [*chanting with delight*]: They're coming past the shrimping pools, they're climbing up the shingle.

GRANDFATHER: I can't see. She was such a pretty little girl too, she used to clamber all in and out of the shrimping pools. And he was such a nice boy when he came to stay here with us, and they'd go off down to the sea in the evening and I'd try not to watch because it didn't seem fair to watch, but I couldn't help it, I went all the way down to the sea with them, holding hands and kicking at the sand. I could feel the water round their ankles, though I was too far away even to see their ankles I suppose. We were so happy.

TIM: Mum-my! Dad-dy! Come on! Can't they hear me? They haven't even waved. Ooooheeee! Now Daddy's waving. Now Mummy's waving. Now they're in the sand-dunes, Mummy's slipping and Daddy's pulling her up, now they're coming. Now I can't see them, they've come on to the road. They're nearly here, they're just coming along the road. Why don't you look? They're at the gate, they're coming up the steps from the road. Here they are now, here they are! Daddy, Daddy –

STEWART: Hello, Tim, hey, up you go. You're getting a heavy boy. Give us a kiss then.

TIM: Mummy, hello, Mummy.

JANE: Yes, Tim, all right. Don't jump like that, calm down, we've something to tell you.

STEWART: Jane –

JANE: Daddy and I have been having a talk –

STEWART: Tim, listen, old man, it's like this. Mummy and I –

JANE: I'm talking to him, you can't stop me, now be quiet for once.

TIM: I saw you on the beach. I watched you coming.

JANE: Tim, you already understand something of what's been going on, don't you? Though we haven't said anything about it.

TIM: I saw you slip in the sand, did you see me?

STEWART: Tim, I've been away a lot this summer, so I haven't seen as much of you as I wanted –

JANE: You've liked this summer, haven't you, Tim?

TIM: Yes.

STEWART: But in the winter you may live with me or if you live with Mummy you'll see me a lot, won't that be nice?

TIM: Yes.

JANE: Tim, you know your father isn't living with us any more, and now we've decided for always he won't be living with us any more –

STEWART: Jane, stop it, that's a mad way to do it.

JANE: – and you're going to live with me and Uncle Peter.

STEWART: Jane, will you be quiet.

    [*Pause.*]

TIM: Grandpa –

STEWART: Tim, listen to me a minute. It's not as bad as all that. It's fun, you'll have three houses to live in –

JANE: You're living with me. And you must tell anyone who asks you that that's what you're doing and that's what you want to do, do you understand? Now, who do you want to live with? With Mummy, don't you?

TIM: I want to live by myself.

STEWART: We're not sure who you'll be living with, Tim, but whoever it is you'll see the other one lots and lots, as often as you like, and you'll spend all the time you want by the sea with Grandpa –

JANE: Shut up! Tim, if they say do you want to live with Daddy, you must say no, because Daddy left us, Daddy left us alone, long before Uncle Peter came, didn't he, darling?

STEWART: Jane, it's not true –

JANE: You left me long before –

STEWART: I left you because of him –

JANE: I only went to him because you didn't love me, do you think I would have otherwise?

STEWART: You'd been looking at him for months.

JANE: Do you think I would have loved him?

STEWART: That's why I got out and left you to it –

JANE: You pretend you didn't leave till you left for good, but you'd been gone before that, days and days you spent away –

STEWART: Oh, don't let's have it all again.

JANE: – because you didn't love me, you never loved, you left me first, didn't he, Dad?

STEWART: Jane, we've had it all so many times.

JANE [*crying by now*]: Didn't he, Tim? He left us, he left us first –

TIM: Don't cry! Don't you cry! I hate you! Don't cry! Don't!

STEWART: Tim –

TIM: I hate you! Ant! Ant! Ant! [*He cries.*]

JANE [*still cries*].

STEWART: Oh, to hell with this. I'll phone you. [*He goes.*]

    [*Pause.*]

JANE: Stewart. Stewart, wait. [*Her voice is fainter as she follows him into the house. The car starts and goes. She calls again.*]

TIM [*still sniffs and sobs*].

GRANDFATHER: Come on, Tim! Let's find something to do. It's all right, they've all gone away, we're all alone now. All alone and it's getting dark. Now I know what we'll do, I'll just go to the garage, you wait there like a good boy, all by yourself, all right? You watch the sea and tell me if the lighthouse has started up yet, all right? You count how long it is between the flashes. [*He goes, leaving* TIM *looking over the rail.*]

TIM: You ant you. Live by myself. I'll fly in a plane. There it is. One, two, three. You go away. Four, five. One, two. I'll fly away in a plane. Don't cry, I hate you. One two three four five.

GRANDFATHER: Now come on, Tim, this is what we'll do. Can you see where the ants are in the dark? You can just see, can't you? Pour a little petrol on them, that's right. Now we put the string here in the petrol and bring the end way over here so we can shelter from the blast, all right? Down we crouch, then, oh. Now we light the string, here, see, light the string. [*He strikes a match.*] You take the match, you do it. That's right. Blow out the match. Now you wait, the string will burn all the way down to the enemy, see the little flame go all the way down to the ants.

[*The petrol explodes into flame.*]

TIM [*shrieks with laughter*].

END

JEREMY SANDFORD

The Whelks and the Chromium

A SEASIDE ROMANCE

The Whelks and the Chromium was first broadcast in the B.B.C. Third Programme on 4 November 1958 with the following cast:

THE SPIELER	Howard Marion Crawford
RON	Harry Fowler
JOCK	Frank Partington
ANDY	Gerald Fox-Salaman
DI	Denise Bryer
GLADYS	Sheila Grant
PHOTOGRAPHER	William Eedle
OTHER PARTS:	Kara Aldridge
	Hugh Manning
	David March
	David Spenser
	Anthony Viccars
	Harold Young

Produced by Francis Dillon

The author later developed this theme into a full-length stage play, *Dreaming Bandsmen*.

ACT ONE

SCENE ONE

Sea sounds and a juke box playing 'Love me'. Distantly we hear the SPIELER, *mouthing through his execrable mike, smarmily, monotonously, never letting up for a moment.*

SPIELER: Hullo hullo hullo now can everyone hear me can everyone hear me?

Step forward please, step forward now there is others that's wanting to listen.

Come along now, step forward you there, come along right up to the platform.

Step forward please now I want you to step forward please now because there is others that's wanting to listen. . . .

[*He addresses a small crowd of stragglers he has collected.*]

Good evening. And may I address to each and all and everyone of you present tonight a most hearty welcome what has seen fit to do us the honour here on the famed Silver Acre of the Golden Furlong of sunny Southpool on the foaming ocean. I thank you. Now it isn't often that I address you people and in the course of this evening's entertainment I shall be a having quite innumerous items the which to inform you of this the famed Silver Acre in the centre of which Alf's Premier Super Amusements chances to be situate Alf's me by the way.

[*The stragglers murmur, impressed.*]

I thank you. Not only will you be thrilling to our very large number of amusement items and amenities, Butovues, Wallmachines, Juba-phones, Jumbophinds, Skiddophun, What The Butler Saw, Rock-eterias, and What Have You. Not only will you be lingering on the pier in breezes that have been known to sweep the promenade at speeds up to and including forty mile per hour. Not only will you be wandering at your own sweet will entirely through the six square miles of energy and imagination here concentrated before you in concrete form. In addition to this we shall be terminating our evening's entertainment with a visit to the Nineteen Sexty Phun girls, now this is the sexational show that contains more controversial talk-provoking fantastical fictional facets than any other. Banned no less than three times in Birmingham, this is the show that was closed by the policewoman at Brynwyn Falls and that eighteen Carnarvon housewives would not see. It is, and this we may safely say without exaggeration, the NE PLUS ULTRA modern sensation in 3 D sex.

[*The stragglers applaud. Enter* KEN, *a spindly drunk bandsman, and* JOSH, *a shorter built, big-hearted bandsman, preceded by* ANDY, *a spare skirmishing bandsman. All wear magnificent uniforms.*]

SPIELER: I thank you.

[KEN *approaches the* SPIELER, *drunkenly circumnavigates him.*]

KEN: Aw Shute!

JOSH [*appalled*]: Hey, Kennie!

STRAGGLERS: Oi oi!

KEN: Shute!

SPIELER: Now it isn't often that I address to –

KEN: Shute! Shut up!

MAN [*remonstrating*]: I mean, give 'im a chance!

BOY [*pouf's voice*]: I say, steady on there!

JOSH: Turn it in, Ken!

SPIELER: Now it isn't often that I address a –

LARGE WOMAN: Hey, stop that! Sauce!

SPIELER: Now it isn't – yeah, pipe down there if you don't mind please, some of us up here got a job of work to do.

MAN: 'Ere 'ere!

WRESTLER [*strolling up to* KEN]: Watch it! [*He stands threateningly.*]

[KEN *is rescued by the* SPIELER, *who now continues:*]

SPIELER: Oh it's all right, leave 'im be leave 'im be. Well, only I like to see the young fellows enjoying theyselves, don't you? Only we can't enjoy ourselves all the time that's all enit in this harsh world of ours. Well, let's have a giggle, shall we? This bloke in uniform which seems to have such an awful lot to say for his self. Let's let him have a go, eh? Supposing he steps up here beside me –

STRAGGLERS: Aha!

JOSH: He's talkin' to you, Ken.

KEN: Oh no.

SPIELER: That's right, you there.

MAN: Go on, mate.

WOMAN: 'Ave a go, dear.

SPIELER: Because, sir, this is your life. Now just tell us what you find of note –

KEN [*springing up beside him*]: All right I will then! I'll tell you, I find it all of note. The Mums and Dads sipping tea in their raincoats, the spray drifting in clouds over the conveniences, the swinging Scenic with its cargo of hysterics, the rain –

SPIELER: Ah, you see the rain, do you?

KEN: Yeah, and the ravers, wedged into their jeans, come all hot and spending furious from the little towns down the line with razor-blades in their pockets, and the lasses, the cuddlehungry misses, all sweetly displayed, and the tide at the slack, and on the sand old bodies lying, some on the *News of the World*, some on the *Pictorial*, so now friends let's go. Let's lose ourselves in the laugheteria. Disappear into the lavatories and come out years later bemused with old bus tickets sticking to our pants! Let's go where the clouds mass low and red with the neon!

[*To the astonishment of the* SPIELER, KEN *leads the crowd forward now, and as they go they are accosted by the following*]:

BINGOMAN: I say I say I say. You there, you sir, you sir. Now I want two sportsmen, two real sportsmen.

HORSEY HORSEY GIRL: Horsey Horsey! Horsey Horsey! [*She wears jockey's colours and cap, very short shorts.*]

JOSH [*ignoring* BINGOMAN]: Well I said to him, see what ah mean, I said you been drinkin' you have, you been drinkin' too much of that Sarchpedallo.

ANDY [*making strange gestures at* HORSEY HORSEY GIRL]: Marvellous!

SEAGULL CAPT.: Two-thirty for an authentic cruise round the bay, take your seats now, visiting mudflats.

WOMAN: Well, I said sauce. Sauce I said, sauce.

DECKCHAIRMAN: Deckchairs, deckchairs, deckchairs, deckchairs! [*A straggling body of sailors approaches.*]

SAILOR: Right, stand up straight then, and try to make it a lovely show for Southpool. [*The sailors march comically. One of them shouts 'Left left left left!'*]

SAILOR [*exasperated*]: Oh come along, boys. If it's worth doing well it's worth doing well! [*One of the sailors falls out, seems about to be sick.*]

JOSH: See what ah mean, it's what they know by the old jingo of asphixicating.

WOMAN: Where we goin' anyway?

PHOTOGRAPHER: Now who'd like to be photographed in the authentic grass Hawaiian raffia skirt? Come along, ladies, come and be done, you sir, would you like to be done in the old grass skirt?

ANDY [pouf's voice]: Oh yes, mate, thank you very much, mate, oh yes I would so much like to be done in your grass skirt, *get out of it!*

[*Drunken sailor is sick. The marching sailors disintegrate, it seems that it was only their quasi-military formation that was keeping them in control, they stagger about, causing havoc among the more righteous crowd which is following* KEN.]

SAILOR II [sings]: 'Ow can you measure the moon on the scree?

SAILOR: Not 'ere.

DRUNK SAILOR: It was them whelks. Oh!

GRANMA: Whip first, then the Scenic.

GRANPA [angry]: Naow, first the Scenic, then the Whip!

SAILOR II: 'Ow can you fathom the fish in the sea.
        For I like 'em in blue and I like 'em in red
        But far best of all dears I like 'em in . . .

SEAGULL CAPT.: Three-thirty for an authentic cruise round the bay visiting neighbouring mudflats and also the *Ben Nevis*, a ship of some fourteen tons named after the mountain you saw on TV three-thirty for . . .

[*But now* ANDY *puts a coin in the juke box, it lights up to orange and plays, drowning all else, and the crowds follow* KEN *into the limitless distance of the fairground and only* ANDY *remains* . . .]

SCENE TWO

A ROBOT *erupts into maniacal laughter.*

ROBOT: [wild laughter. It lights up. Its eyebrows rise up and down. A beetle begins its endless course round his head. Wild laughter.]

[*Enter* GLADYS *and* DI. GLADYS *giggles in company with the robot out of sheer good spirits.*]

GLADYS: Oh, Di!

DI: What, Glad?

GLAD: See that man? Laughing? [GLAD *is seventeen, with a tawny mass of untidy hair, prettyish.*]

LAUGHER: Aha ha ha ha. Aha ha ha ha.

GLAD: Oops! Listen to him! What in the world's got into him! Did you see him, Di? Di! See that man inside the winder?

[DI *looks. She's older, and not so pretty.*]

DI: That's not a man, silly.

GLAD: Eh? What is he then?

DI: Not a man, at any rate.

GLAD: What is 'e then?

DI: That's a sculptor.

GLAD: Oh. [*Pause.*] I know.

DI: Well, all right, I was only telling you.

GLAD: I'm not that daft.

LAUGHER [*laughs*].

GLAD [*unable not to join in, giggles again, then says*]: Oh, Di –

DI: What is it now?

GLAD: I can't stop laughing myself!

DI: Oh you. [*When* GLAD *and the* ROBOT *have finished she adds*] That's cos it's a Happidrome, Glad. See? That's what a Happidrome is.

[*Again* ROBOT *and* GLAD *erupt into laughter.*]

GLAD: Oh, Di, it's happening again!

DI: Oh go on with you.

[GLAD *stops.*]

Hey, look at this.

[GLAD *giggles quietly.*]

Oh you. No, look.

GLAD: What?

DI: This, silly.

[*It's a slot machine. Other slot machines present include Weighing Machine, The Bare Idea and It Happened One Night, Haunted Churchyard and a punch ball.*]

GLAD [*obligingly*]: Coo.

DI: 'Cupid's Secrets.' Shall I read it?

GLAD: Might as well.

DI: 'Push penny in slot, grip handle, and squeeze gently together.'
   [GLAD *giggles*.]
  'The barometer will then record your amorous propensities.'
  Well!

GLAD: Let's have a go!

DI: O.K.! You got a penny?

GLAD: Half a sec. Yeah. There.

DI: Well then, put it in. Yeah. There.

GLAD: What, in there?

DI: That's right. In there.

GLAD [*trying*]: Won't go.

DI: Won't go? What's wrong then?

GLAD: Dunno.

DI: Let's have a look. Oh no, it doesn't go in there, silly.

GLAD: Why not?

DI: In there! Where it says 'coin ejector'.
   [GLAD *giggles*.]
  Now come along, you tell me what's funny about that?

GLAD [*giggles*]: Coin ejector!

DI: Oh you're daft. Now come along. Push it in. There!
   [*Coin drops.*]

GLAD [*pause*]: What now?

DI [*happy but embarrassed*]: Um, well, er squeeze together.

GLAD: Oh. O.K.

DI [*about to take the plunge*]: All right.
   [*They embrace.*]

BOTH: Mmmmmmmmmmmmmmmmmmmmmmmmmmmmmmmmm!
   [GLAD *sighs contentedly*.]

DI [*pause*]: Hey, Glad.

GLAD [*faintly*]: Yes, Di?

DI: Nice like this. Think so?

GLAD: Like . . . what?

DI: Like . . . this.

GLAD: Mmm. All right.

DI: I'll say.

GLAD: Wish you was somebody else, Di.

DI [*springing away*]: Oh Glad, that spoils it.

GLAD: Well of all the – what's wrong with you?

LAUGHER [*laughs*].

DI: Oh, I dunno.

GLAD: No, what's wrong with you, Di? Why did you spring away like that?

DI [*angry*]: I told you. I *dunno*.

GLAD [*her turn to be hurt*]: Well!

DI: I think it's silly anyways. Is that all it does?

GLAD: It ain't done nothing yet!

DI: Oh no, nor it hasn't.

GLAD: You'd of thought they'd make it do *something*.

DI: Praps. Praps we weren't squeezed hard enough?

GLAD: Well, what d'you expect, springing away like that?

DI: Oh, shut your trap!

GLAD [*upset*]: What's come over you? Di?

LAUGHER [*laughs*].

DI: Oh forget it, Glad. Just, I was wondering . . .

GLAD [*pause*]: What? Di?

LAUGHER [*laughs*].

GLAD: What, Di? Thinking we ought to try again?

DI: All right, Glad.

   [*They embrace again.*]

GLAD [*after a pause, sadly*]: Not working at all this time, Glad, I'm afraid.

DI: Mm. No.

GLAD: Maybe we ought ter shake it?

   [GLAD *disengages.*]

DI: Could be, Glad. All right. You take that there.

GLAD: Yes?

DI: Got it tight? All right, shake! That's right. Now. Harder! Harder!

GLAD: Oh! Oh!

   [*Strange noises from inside machine.*]

DI: Don't stop! Go on! Harder!

GLAD: Oh look, it's working!

DI: Can't be!

GLAD: Yes, the barometer, look!

DI: Oh yes, it's beginning to rise!

GLAD: What's it say, look!

DI: Look what it says, look!

   [*A loud bubbling noise comes from inside machine.*]

GLAD [*reading*]: Cuddlesome
　　　　　　　Lovable
BOTH:　　　　Courteous
　　　　　　　Curvatious
　　　　　　　Kissable
　　　　　　　Bashful
　　　　　　　Beauteous
　　　　　　　Flirty
　　　　　　　Flighty
　　　　　　　Sultry
　　　　　　　Saucy
　　　　　　　Sexational
　　　　　　　BOOPS!

[*The juke goes green, strikes up with 'Love Me'. GLAD and DI jump up and down, laughing and clapping to the music.*]

DI: Boops! That's us, Glad, enit, boops!

GLAD: Boops! Di, boops, boops, boops!

DI: Boops, did you see what it said, Glad?

GLAD: Boops! It said boops, did you see, Di?

DI: Boops, it said boops boops boops boops!

GLAD: Boops, boops, boops, boops!

LAUGHER [*tumultuous laughter*].

[*Music climax, then pull down and hold under what follows.*]

SCENE THREE

Enter JOSH *and* KEN. ANDY *still standing by the robot.*

ANDY: Hey boys, boys!

KEN: Hi, Andy.

ANDY: Boys, you just missed something!

JOSH: What was that, Andy?

ANDY: Two bints playin' around. They was just – *there!*

KEN: Playing around? What were they doin' then?

ANDY: Well, playing around!

JOSH: Well, where are they?

ANDY: Playing around! Marvellous!

JOSH: Well, where are they?

ANDY: Oh, I dunno. [*Sidetracked by a slot machine.*]

JOSH: You know something, Ken?

KEN: What's that, Josh?

JOSH: That new hairstyle of yours is reminiscent of Elvis Presley. See what ah mean, Ken?

KEN: Think so?

JOSH: Straight. Well, you won't be wearin' that much longer, eh, Ken?

KEN: Not me.

JOSH: Really disgustin' gettin' up on that stage with that bloke, eh, Andy?

ANDY: Eh? Oh marvellous, yeah, absolutely.

JOSH: Though I still maintain, Ken, you know what I think?

KEN: It wasn't that made me drunk.

ANDY: What was it then?

KEN: Sickness.

JOSH: Eh?

ANDY: Oh, absolutely. Hm, wish I could rid me of them blackheads. They're a curse.

JOSH: I can't see any.

ANDY [*ruefully*]: Oh, them's there.

JOSH: Did you try that advert I give you from *Startling Detective*?

ANDY: Marvellous! I sent but they ain't replied yet. It really is most provoking. Well it's not for meself I mind like, it's the other sex.

JOSH: I follow.

ANDY: What would you do if you was with fifteen women on a desert island? Ho! marvellous! [*He leaps about, carried away by his imagination.*]

JOSH: Well, makes a change from the old bandroom, eh, Andy?

SCENE FOUR

Re-enter GLADYS *and* DI.

GLADYS: Which you usin', magic curve line?

DI: Same as always.

GLAD: Hm. Suits you. Did you read, what was it, *Imprudent Love*?

DI: No.

GLAD: Oh, we won't be bored anyway.

DI: Why?

GLAD: There's a juke.

DI: Oh.

GLAD: Let's have a tune eh. What shall we have, Di?

DI: Well, what about your usual?

GLAD: What usual?

DI: Oh, don't come that on me, you know. The solo.

GLAD: Oh yes!

DI: Don't give me that, you were planning that all along.

GLAD: No I wasn't.

DI: Oh, here we go again. By the way, did you see that in *True Romances* about that old grandshah or whatever he was?

GLAD [*absently*]: Can't say I did.

DI: Well this grandshah see he chooses all his brides from snapshots.

GLAD: From snapshots? Well how many does he have then?

DI: This will astonish you. Nineteen.

GLAD: Shall I put it on?

DI: What?

GLAD: It. The solo.

DI: Oh solo solo solo solo, you'll be turning into a solo shortly.

GLAD: Well, it was your suggestion.

DI: Wouldn't be surprised you turned into a solo one day. All right, I'm not stopping you.

GLAD: Though, you know, he played it better than the bloke on this.

DI: You're entitled to that opinion, Glad.

GLAD: Well, didn't he?

DI: 'Course he did. Still no news?

GLAD: Absolutely nil.

DI: There's a pity.

GLAD: Five weeks now. Well, maybe it was the end of the season see. Winter come after when they keep 'em locked up.

DI: So 'e couldn't of got out, even if 'e tried.

GLAD: Could of climbed.

DI: Still maintain you should of written him.

GLAD: So I would of but I didn't know his name.

DI: Awkward.

GLAD: I'd of felt silly writing just –

DI: Mm.

GLAD: And them blokes, you know, they got ever such a sense of humour.

DI: Just when you'd found someone really romantic.

GLAD: He'll be back.

DI: Think so?

GLAD: It's the spring now. Almost. Shall I tell you a secret?

DI [*hastily*]: Oh do, Glad, do, Glad!

GLAD: I did write him.

DI: You wrote him?

GLAD: Yeah.

DI: You wrote him? Saying what?

GLAD: Just – isn't that what you said I should?

DI: Oh, *Glad* –

GLAD: What?

DI: Shouldn't of done it –

GLAD: Why?

DI: Boys don't like it!

GLAD: Don't they?

DI: Boys don't like that!

GLAD: But I was getting –

DI: It's the very worst thing you could possibly of done.

GLAD [*weeping*]: Oh, Di, was it?

DI: You've burnt your boats, that's quite clear.

GLAD: Did I frighten him off? Oh, Di, you might show a bit of sympathy.

DI: Oh no. No, don't get worked up. I didn't mean it like that. Oh no. No, I'm sure he'll come, anyway, how could it of got there, he'll come.

GLAD: Think he will?

DI: Yeah!

GLAD: Sure?

DI: Course he will. Now, let's put on your disc. There. [*She puts coin in juke.*]

GLAD: All right, Di. And, Di –

DI: What?

GLAD: Don't look at me.

[DI *walks off apart. Music begins. Cornet solo begins, Carnival of Venice.* GLADYS *sings to tune, then dreams.*]

117

GLADYS: Darling . . . Darling . . . I love you so my dear . . . how well you trilled, remember, how well you slurred, how perfect your markatos and pizzicatos and wandering wonderful crescendos. . . . It was the first concert I'd ever been to and there you were in the bandstand with all the other bandsmen, playing away on their instruments and you playing louder than all of them. And you know, from the very first moment I went there I got the feeling you'd noticed me. I noticed you, you with your bugle. And afterwards when you'd finished and you come up through the crowds to introduce yourself and oh I was all of a tremble I was ever so excited, and then the music from the dancehall and then on the beach when you whispered, I can't hear I said. Then you moved in closer, I could feel your breath on my neck and I was silly, wasn't I? I said 'Whatever are you doing?' But I soon got to like it all right. Not that I'd let you have your way now, Ken, because it wasn't so very sensible of me, was it? One more fervid embrace in the spray from the pier, then, *Praps I might see you HOME!!!!!!* Oh, it weren't half wonderful. When we got back, quietly so as not to wake my Dad, all of a sudden without any warning, but for further reflection there was no time because, Darling darling, my love, my true one, how well you trilled remember, how well you slurred, how perfect your markatos and pizzicatos and wandering wonderful crescendos!

[*Juke box climax and finish.*]

SCENE FIVE

Enter ANDY *and* JOSH.

ANDY: Lovely sands, don't you think, Josh?

JOSH: Eh, Andy?

ANDY: I said, lovely sands.

JOSH: Oh, aye.

ANDY: 'We don't know when we're lucky.'

JOSH: How long till parade?

ANDY: Hour. Makes a change from the old bandroom, eh, Josh? Oh look.

JOSH: What?

ANDY: Slotbox.

JOSH: 'Haunted Churchyard'. You got a penny?

ANDY: Here y'are.

JOSH [*puts in coin*]: And there she goes!
    [*The machine hums.*]
  Look at that, boy! Hey, look at that! Wow!

ANDY: Look at that bloke there!

JOSH: Look at – Wow!

BOTH [*inarticulate cries and whistles*].
    [*The whirring stops.*]

JOSH: Oh.

ANDY: That's the end.

JOSH: What next?

ANDY: Hey, Josh?

JOSH: Eh?

ANDY: There's them bints.

JOSH: Bints? Where?

ANDY: Them two over there. By the juke box.

JOSH: Oh yes. So they are.

ANDY: What you think of them?

JOSH: All right.

ANDY: How 'bout pickin' them up?

JOSH: Oh, no.

ANDY: Marvellous! Why not?

JOSH: Wouldn't stand a chance.

ANDY: Why not?

JOSH: Oh look, that's interestin'.

ANDY: What's that?

JOSH: 'The bare idea, some innocence exposed for adults only.'

ANDY: Oh.

JOSH: Come on. Put in the money. [*He inserts coin. Again they gaze, with inarticulate cries.*]

JOSH: Wow, that was very interestin'. See what ah mean, Andy?

ANDY: Them bints is still there, Josh.

JOSH: Now let's look if there's any – hey, why you keep lookin' at them bints over there?

ANDY: Let's have a go, Josh.

JOSH: Why? See what ah mean, Andy?

ANDY: Them things has kind of inspired me.

JOSH: I follow. Do you really want to?

ANDY: Yeah.

JOSH: I follow. Well, what's stoppin' you?

ANDY: Yeah, but how?

JOSH: Well, just go in, get talkin'.

ANDY: You must come too, though.

JOSH: They're not my type.

ANDY: I can't go alone.

JOSH: Why not?

ANDY: I can't. Come on, Josh.

JOSH: No. I'm not coming.

ANDY: Why not?

JOSH: 'Cos we'll get our heads snapped off, that's why. They're that type.

ANDY: Well, I'm going anyhow.

JOSH: All right. Carry on. But don't say I didn't warn you!

ANDY [*slight pause*]: Ain't you comin'? [*Then, with relief.*] Oh, it's too late.

JOSH: Too late my eye. What you mean?

ANDY: Well, they've got up. They're going.

JOSH: Going my foot! After them! Stop them! If you really want them, that is.

ANDY: But how?

JOSH: Shout something to attract their attention.

ANDY: What?

JOSH: Anything.

ANDY: Hey! You there! You over there!

JOSH: Oh no!

[*Exit* ANDY, *followed by* JOSH. *Enter* GLAD *and* DI *followed by* ANDY.]

ANDY: You there! You there!

DI: Oh, Glad!

ANDY: I say! You there!

[*Re-enter* JOSH.]

You there!

DI: Glad!

GLAD: What?

DI: They're after us!

GLAD: What?

DI: Them blokes! They're after us. How do I look? [*Adopts pin-up position.*]

GLAD: Oh you!

ANDY [*seeing pin-up before him*]: Wow! Gee! Crazy! Grand! Gee! Marvellous!

DI [*to* JOSH]: Was you by any chance talkin' to me?

ANDY: Well yes, I er –

DI: Well, who do you think you are, bawling away –

JOSH [*smoothly*]: We was wonderin' whether you and your friend would care to come for a stroll.

GLAD: Oh.

DI: Oh no.

JOSH: What you mean, no?

DI: No, we don't do that.

JOSH: Don't do what?

DI: Stroll as you call it. We don't go in for that sort of thing.

JOSH: What sort of thing? Where was you going to anyway?

DI: Since when has that been any business of yours?

GLAD: Are you by any chance suggesting an alternative?

ANDY: Well, I hadn't anythin' in mind but –

JOSH: We was wonderin' whether you'd care to come, have a look at the Nineteen Sexty Phun girls.

ANDY: After that there's a concert you might care to –

DI: Hey, Glad –

GLAD: Yeah.

DI: Don't like these boys very much.

GLAD: No.

DI: Only thing is, not wearing the same things as your bloke was, are they?

GLAD: Could be. It was dark. Oh no, I don't think so. 'E was smarter.

DI: Well, you see such a lot of uniforms these days. Do you want to carry through with it?

GLAD: Well no, not very much, I mean, Ken might come.

DI: He wouldn't be scared of them.

GLAD: No, but 'e might be put off.

DI: Better ditch 'em.

GLAD: Yeah, but how?

DI: I dunno. Somehow. Leave it to me, Glad.

JOSH: Er, excuse me –

GLAD [*hysterical with excitement*]: No, look, look over there, that's him, that's him!

JOSH: Pardon?

[*But* GLAD *is already away at full tilt. Music.*]

SCENE SIX

KEN: So! It's you!

GLAD: Me!

KEN: Where did you spring from? I never expected –

GLAD: Oh, why didn't you say you was comin', why did you never answer my letters? What you been doin' since I saw you, oh why didn't you let me know, what's your name, oh how are you –

KEN: Now, my girl, one question at a time please!

[JOSH *places finger over his lips, mysteriously draws* ANDY *away.*]

KEN [*not yet involved with her, not really wanting to be left alone with her*]: Hey, you two, it's all right, don't leave us.

JOSH [*returning, patting* KEN *on the shoulder style of conspirator*]: See what ah mean, Ken? I understand, Ken.

[GLAD *comes up to* KEN, *stands against him, arms round his neck, on tiptoe.*]

KEN: You look good, Gladys.

GLAD: Why did you never come back to see me?

KEN: I'm sorry, I was –

GLAD: Why didn't you let me know you was comin' today?

KEN: I didn't know your address – I'm getting demobbed tomorrow, I just didn't think –

GLAD: Demobbed? What do you mean? You goin' away?

KEN: As far as London.

GLAD: Listen, you can't. What's your name?

KEN: Ken.

GLAD: Well, Ken, you can't. I'm telling you.
  [*Re-enter* JOSH.]

KEN: Who's the girl-friend, Glad?

GLAD: Oh, she's –

DI: Well, Ken, I'm Di. I don't expect you remember, I was there last time but –

KEN: Sure. This is my mate, Josh.

DI: Hi, Josh.

JOSH: We've met.

KEN: And that's Andy.

ANDY: Marvellous!

GLAD: Ken, Ken Ken Ken Ken, it sounds funny, Kenny, you know that solo you played, you know, that night, you know. [*She sings.*]

KEN: What's that? Oh is that the Carnival? I know. D'you remember it?

GLAD: You bet. I been playin' that disc ever since, almost.

KEN: Didn't know it was on a disc, who's playing it?

GLAD: You know where I play it? On the juke. But you know, I think you play it better than the bloke on that disc.

KEN [*amused yet pleased*]: Do you?

GLAD: I do, Ken.

KEN: That hat, what you got written on it?

GLADYS: 'Kiss me.'

JOSH: See what ah mean . . . [*He ushers* DI *away.*]

KEN: What?

GLAD: 'Kiss me.'
  [KEN *kisses her.*]
  [*More intimately.*] I think you could of read that without me telling you.

KEN: Do you?

GLAD: What you been doin' since I saw you, Ken, really, thought you was dead or something, 'ave you got a girl-friend?

KEN: I did have.

GLAD [taking his hand, swinging it]: Did have. That's good.

KEN: Now, let's see if I read that message right.

GLAD: Better come and make sure, didn't you?

[KEN approaches but she runs away. Picking up litter basket she throws it at him. He catches her.]

Oh look, Ken, look at the Scenic, up there –

[As he looks she whips his hat, breaks away.]

KEN: Hey! You! Give us the cap! Look, I can be charged! [He chases her, catches her, and they wrestle for the cap. At length she is forced to relinquish it.]

GLAD: All right, I'll give it you back.

[Enjoying the game he continues.]

I said – I'll give it you back!

[KEN, disappointed, takes it.]

JOSH [worried]: Hey, Ken –

KEN: Yes?

JOSH: May I suggest?

KEN: What?

JOSH: May I suggest there is people watching you?

KEN: There's nobody watching.

JOSH: There is you know.

ANDY: Hey boys, look!

JOSH: What?

ANDY: Look boys, look!

JOSH: 'Moloch will tell.'

[It is a vast great machine, squatting like a God with its analysing tubes.]

ANDY: You ask it questions, grand gee, wow, will I be a film star, will I get a rise, gee, crazy! Will I get a rise?

[He grasps analysing tube. Barometer contraption boils up. The machine says, with a loud whirr, absolutely mechanically]:

MOLOCH: NO!

ANDY: You! [He kicks machine.] Will I hit the big time?

MOLOCH: NO!

ANDY: [Spars with machine]: Listen to this, boys: Have I sex appeal?

MOLOCH: NO!

[*Exit* ANDY.]

JOSH: Have a go. 'Will the little stranger be a boy?'

DI: Oh, what a peculiar question!

MOLOCH: NO!

JOSH: Oh, it's rigged. See what ah mean, Ken?

DI [*to* KEN]: What was wrong with your friend, by the way?

GLAD: Ken, now you go on the doodah!

KEN: Me? I don't trust it.

GLAD: Try, Ken.

KEN: Hm. 'Will I get what I want?'

GLAD: You have to stand on it, you boob!

KEN: Will I get what I want?

GLAD: Oh Ken. [*Giggles.*]

MOLOCH: YES!

KEN: There you are, see!

JOSH: Great!

DI: Well I never.

GLAD [*quietly*]: You will, Ken.

DI: Glad!

JOSH: Come along, Gladys, now, it's your turn.

DI: Don't you go near it, Glad, I don't trust it one inch, I can tell you.

GLAD: No, I want to. Half a sec., here I come. Here I am. There. I'll have – What sort of questions can I ask? Oh, I see. 'Will my luck change? Will I ever get a rise? Will I be a film star, will I be rich, will I be happy?' Oh, Di – [*romantically*]: 'Will my dreams come true?' [*She works machine. It whirrs as before, but no word is spoken.*]

DI: Why didn't it answer?

JOSH: Peculiar.

KEN [*kicks machine*]: That's strange.

GLAD: Why didn't it answer me? Why didn't it answer me? Why didn't it answer me? [*She bursts into tears. All comfort her. Juke box strikes up.*]

A heavy gong sounds. The curtains of the 'Nineteen Sexty Phun girls'
part. SPIELER *steps out with his mike.* GLAD *and* KEN *watch, embraced.*

SPIELER: Good evening. And now, as earlier promised you, a visit
to the Nineteen Sexty Phun girls, the up-to-date controversial
show that contains more talk provoking fictional facets than anything else on the esplanade. This is the show that we may well call
and rightly. Now in the course of our show tonight you will be
seeing not only. In addition to this. Just one request. When our
phun girls come on to the stage make no comment. The creature
the which you are about to see before you is the child of sin. I
thank you. [*He strikes a gong. The curtains part to show Blondie.*]
I thank you. This creature which you see before you was married.
She was unable to enjoy the pleasures of Motherhood for reasons
which I cannot here relate. Blondie is racked in the veins, a martyr
to dropsy and the stone, Blondie has no feet. I thank you. [*He strikes
gong. Curtains close.*]

GLADYS: Oh, Ken, it's terrible!

SPIELER: Now when Blondie first left the north for London marks
the commencement of this tragic tale of civilian corruption and
woe. At that time Blondie was a fine outstanding lass like many
another. [*He strikes gong. Curtains open.*] *How* innocent she looks,
with the whole wild world stretching before her. Or so she thought.
I thank you. [*He hits gong. Curtains close.*] But how wrong she was
the poor little innocent. In our next study we see her already far
gone down the primrose path. I thank you. [*He hits gong. Curtains
open.*] In her hand you will notice what is in appearance a cigarette.
In fact she is indulging in a reefer or, put it another way, a drug-
soaked drag. I thank you. [*He hits gong. Curtains close.*] And now
yet further misfortune is dogging the feet of the hapless lass. Her
face is daubed with powder and lipstick. She has gravitated, sunk
through the sieve. In her hand you will observe a telephone. But
now she is not a stone's throw away from Europe's sin-centre –
[*He hits gong. Curtains open.*] Chelsea.

MEMBER OF AUDIENCE: Tut tut. Poor little thing. Shouldn't ever
of left the north.

SPIELER: I thank you. [*He hits gong. Curtains close.*]

ANDY: Hey, but Mister, where was the telephone?

SPIELER: What, didn't you see no bloomin' telephone?

ANDY: I didn't see no bloomin' telephone.

KEN: No, nor me neither.

SPIELER: Well, where *were* you looking! [*Laughs horribly, and at length. Great surge of music.*]

SCENE EIGHT

The entrance to the 'River Caves'. Enter KEN *and* GLAD.

GLAD: But that's for lovers!

KEN: That's right.

GLAD: Oh no, Ken!

KEN: Why not?

[*He goes over to the guichet. Then* GLADYS *follows him.* KEN *pays at the guichet, they go in. And now, amidst darkness, we hear the great surging waltz from Rosenkavalier, played in pop style with echochamber strings.* KEN *and* GLAD *float in a boat through the caves. A cataract to one side makes her lean over towards him.*]

GLAD: Oh, Ken, look! It's water! Streamin' down!

KEN: All right Glad, you'll be all right.

GLAD: Oh, Ken, look at that! As if it was, like – an Egyptian pyramid, like we was inside it. Oh, what's that?

KEN: Stalactites.

GLAD: Satellites!

KEN: It's what you have to hold up the earth. Mind out. More water.

GLAD: Oh, Ken, I have to keep moving over to you because of all this water. Oh help! It's streaming! Oh look, ain't that lovely! Like the South Seas. Look at all them huts! And all them palm trees. Oh and look at the reflection! You can see it all reflected. What's this, a jungle?

KEN: A forest.

GLAD: A forest!

KEN: African.

GLAD: African! Look at that snake!

[*Bird croaks.*]

GLAD: What was that?

KEN: A bird.

GLAD: A bird! Oh look at it, look at its long legs!

[*They embrace.*]

GLAD: You know, Ken, you ought to put something on your hair, Ken, you know that?

KEN: Is that so?

GLAD: Because it's lovely hair you've got, Ken, and I'm not boasting. But it is a shame to keep it like that.

KEN: Is it?

GLAD: Well, after all, there is the long-term proposition to be thought of.

KEN: Will you be my long-term proposition, Glad?

GLAD: Oh, Ken, you are nice, well, I hardly know you. Oh look, look at that old, like, medieval castle. Is that where Nell Gwynne lived?

KEN: Come close, more water!

[*They embrace.*]

SCENE NINE

Enter SERGEANT.

SERG: Right, come along you fellows now, come along, get lined up for the concert, get fell in now, this is Bandsergeant Sousaphone calling all members of the Band of the Royal Bombardiers get fell in get fell in, the concert begins five minutes from now, get fell in if you please in your places in the bandstand, get fell in get fell in. [*Exit* SERGEANT.]

[*Enter* KEN *and* GLADYS.]

GLADYS: You have to go now, Ken, is that what that means?

KEN: 'Fraid so.

GLAD: Who is that silly old man anyway?

KEN: Sergeant.

GLAD: What's a Sergeant?

KEN: I like you.

[*Bandsmen pass on their way to parade.*]

GLAD: So I won't see you any more, Ken?

KEN: Why not?

GLAD: Well, will I?

KEN: You will.

GLAD: Oh good.

KEN: Will you see me tonight, Glad, after the concert?

GLAD: Any time. Oh, I've got a present for you.

[*Bandsmen pass.*]

Well, this one's from my Mum really, she says soldiers are always hungry. Oh, and here's a flower. And here – well – I don't know if you really ought to have it, anyways, here you are, I wrote for it from *Boyfriend*.

KEN: What is it?

GLAD: Just a going steady ring actually.

[*After a moment's hesitation,* KEN *puts it on. Enter* SERGEANT.]

SERG: Right, get fell in all of you, get fell in get fell in, where are you all? Come along now, get fell in in the bandstand, out of it out of it, come along, get fell in now.

[*The last bandsmen go past.* KEN *joins them. They begin to form up in the bandstand.* GLADYS *wistfully watches as the* SERGEANT *forms them up.*]

Right now, come along all of you, we're behindhand now as it is, come along now get formed up get formed up, come along now, Ken Cornet!

BANDMASTER: Prepare to play, Sergeant!

SERG: Band! Attenshun! Prepare to play!

BANDMASTER: Order of Play. First, Carnival of Venice. Soloist Bandsman Ken Cornet.

SERG: Carnival of Venice. After two, one two!

[*The band begins to play. Enter* DI.]

GLAD: Hullo! Di! Di!

DI: Ah, there you are, Glad. How did it go, Glad?

GLAD: Wonderful! Di, do you hear?

DI: What?

GLAD: It's that Carnival. Oh, he's stood up. He's going to do the solo. Oh, look at him, look at him!

MAN: Hey, would you mind, young lady? Only trying to listen to the bloody music.

E 129

GLAD: Yes, but it's my boyfriend!

[KEN *begins the solo.*]

Listen! He's asked me out after, Di. Oh, isn't he smashing! And to think I'll be with him, and he'll be taking my arm, and we'll be walking under the moon, and then he'll be putting his arm round my waist, and his head will be brushing into mine, and then, oh Di, oh Di, I can't *wait*! [*The music swells up loud as she looks towards him.*]

END

ALAN SHARP

The Long-distance Piano-player

A PARABLE FOR RADIO

'all men are fall men and fall men we all are'

The Long-distance Piano-player was first broadcast in the B.B.C. Third Programme on 17 August 1962, with music composed and played by Richard Rodney Bennett, and the following cast:

NARRATOR	Leonard Maguire
THE PIANO-PLAYER	Charles Hodgson
HIS MANAGER	Tom Watson
OTHER VOICES:	Robert Baird Ilsa Cameron
	Michael Deacon Yvonne Gillan
	Alex McCrindle David McKail
	Colin Miller Audrey Muir
	William Simpson Alan Thompson

Percussion by Denis McCarthy

Produced by Christopher Holme

NOTE

In this text the music directions are as the author wrote them. In the B.B.C. production the composer, after being thoroughly briefed by the author, was encouraged to take his own line. A speech tape was recorded first and the music composed directly from it. The music was then recorded, built up electronically, and finally mixed in with the speech and effects in the B.B.C.'s Radiophonic Workshop.

The piano starts to play; the tune is 'You are My Sunshine', and the chorus is played gently until the NARRATOR'S *voice comes in. It is a bland, faintly sardonic tone.*

NARRATOR: He began to play on a bright Tuesday morning and a notice said he would play until the world record had been broken. This stood at present at one hundred and sixty hours and was held, it appeared, by a German.

[*A pause and there is the piano re-establishing the tune, playing for a moment then fading under the* NARRATOR.]

The pianist was a small, rather thin young man who slouched somewhat and played with an economy of movement that made his hands seem two animals engaged in a long mating process, never consummated, never abandoned.

[*The piano increases in volume from the words 'played with . . .' and bridges for a while. The tune is 'The Tennessee Waltz'.*]

He was in a big high room and the piano was in the middle of the floor and ropes had been put around so that the pianist sat in a little arena playing soft boneless tunes to which there didn't seem to be very much point in listening considering how long he had to play.

[*The piano plays on in the above fashion. The tune can be anything slightly lyrical and just a little dated. It pauses after a moment to allow dialogue between two women. They are type voices, one brisk and knowing, the other dull and receptive. The piano plays behind them throughout.*]

He is going to play all week –
How do you mean play all week –
All week, he's going to play all week –
What's he doing it for, what's it for? –
It's a record if he plays all week, he's trying to beat the record –
And he's going to play all week, in there –
They have to feed him everything, his meals and all that –
Won't he stop for anything then? –
There wouldn't be much point if he could stop, that's the whole point not to stop –
I suppose so –

[*The piano fills in until the* NARRATOR.]

At first not many people went in, and those who did stood around

rather sheepishly and waited to see if anything was going to happen.
The pianist did not look at them and after a while their awkwardness
eased and they tried to picture him sitting there while they watched
television and went to the cinema and went to sleep and to work
next morning.

[*Piano fills in for a moment.* NARRATOR.]

Occasionally his manager, a plump little man with gnawed nails,
would come in and speak to the piano-player, muffled, important-
sounding talk.

[*Dialogue between the* MANAGER *and the* PIANIST. *The* MANAGER'S
*voice is that of the professional public relations man, although here
it is not particularly to be emphasized. The* PIANIST *has a certain
small difficulty in articulation and his speech even on the most trivial
matters is fraught with a faint anxiety. The piano plays quite loudly
throughout the whole of the conversation in which the manager speaks
first.*]

I can't find your shirt, the white one –
It's in the travelling bag –
No it's not, I've just looked there –
Are you sure, that's where it was –
I looked just before I came down –
I can't think where it can be unless it's in your case –
What would it be doing in my case? –
Well if it's not in the bag it can only be in your case or with
George's things –
It might be with George's things all right but it's not in my case,
what would it be doing in my case –
I don't know, I could have sworn it was in the bag –

[*The piano takes over and bridges to the* NARRATOR.]

The way in which the manager confers with the pianist always seems
to augur some event. But all that ever happens is that after he has
gone the pianist returns his gaze to some remote corner of the
room and lets his hands scuttle back and forth, like crabs, one tune
blending into another in a long escalator of tedium.

[*The piano comes in and plays a chorus which never quite attains
melodic definition. Under it there is a sound personifying the conveyor-
belt boredom of the performance, a noise irritating but not strident. It
fades for the* NARRATOR.]

There is a billiard saloon across the way and the young men who frequent it find the pianist and his attempt a matter of considerable interest.

[*The voices of the young men are raw and vigorous. Behind them in a high hollow atmosphere the noises of billiard balls and the voices and cues of the players can be heard. Faintly, beyond this, the piano makes thin noises.*]

He'll never play that length of time, it's impossible –

That German did it, didn't he –

I don't believe that –

It was in the papers, there was a photo of him –

That's right they had to take him to hospital –

Exhaustion it was –

Should think so an' all –

Who's to play, the red's hanging? –

[*A lull in the talk and the noises of balls and faint piano, the clicking of the ivories and the dumm of the cushions providing a rhythm section for the sad, distant piano. It goes on for a time then further dialogue.*]

Just think of being awake all that length of time, more than a week–

He won't be awake, when it's quiet he'll get the old head down and the manager or somebody will rattle out a few tunes in case anybody comes past –

No, you can't do that, there's a judge in with him to see he doesn't stop playing –

The judge will be in on it, he'll be getting his cut –

No, it's all fair and above-board, that's why it's for the world record –

World record nothing –

Yes the world record, there's an official judge from the musicians' union or something like that –

Even if he doesn't get a break look at the money he's making –

He's welcome to it, I'd rather have my sleep any day –

You're a lazy bugger though –

I'd give it a bash for what he's getting out of it –

You can't play the piano –

No but if I could –

You wonder who thinks these ideas up –

Well look at those guys who sit on top of poles –

And those dances that go on for days –

That's in America though –

They're mad over there –

[*The piano goes on with its piece, the billiard balls accompanying. After a time the* NARRATOR *comes in.*]

So during the day they play interminable games and watch each other playing, lulled by the chuckle of the balls on the bright baize and soothed by the geometry of random patterns, while with half an ear they listen to this chance accompaniment to their lives, boredom shot through with melancholy.

[*The sounds come in again and play for a while then the billiard hall noise fades and leaves the piano soloing. The tune emerges as 'Time on My Hands'. After the melody has been started a clock strikes, full and slow. There is a pause between chimes and in these pauses the* NARRATOR *speaks, the piano playing with him.*]

Time . . . [CHIME] . . . having nothing else to do . . . [CHIME] . . . passes . . .

[CHIME . . . *and a series of chimes, widely spaced with a ticking noise between and the piano playing quietly, the tune still recognizable. After the last stroke fades the* NARRATOR *comes in.*]

In the morning a number of people looked in to see how the pianist had survived his vigil. The manager greeted them at the entrance.

[*Piano plays behind the* MANAGER'S *voice.*]

Go right in and see him, fresh as when he started, looks better than most of you and he's been up all night, go on in and he'll play a request for you before you go to work.

[*The piano comes up and the* NARRATOR *comes in.*]

Inside there is a large blackboard on an easel and chalked on it are the hours he has been playing and the hours that he has yet to play, so that it can be told at a glance just what the position is and how the balance stands. The manager waits until there are a dozen or so around the arena before drawing attention to the blackboard by tapping it with a short pointer.

[*Sound of tapping, the piano behind. The* MANAGER *in a television advert voice . . .*]

Each day, ladies and gentlemen, we will be posting the morning bulletin on the Marathon Man's condition after he has been examined by a qualified physician. As you see the board has the headings, Blood Pressure, a very important factor that, Temperature, also very important, and Pulse, and this morning we are pleased to announce that these three vital factors are completely normal and that the general condition of the Marathon Man is completely satisfactory.

[*The piano defines into 'I'm Sitting on Top of the World'. It plays a little and the* NARRATOR *comes in.*]

These facts are duly inscribed in chalk by another member of the team and visitors upon reading them now look at the pianist for verification.

[*Piano a little louder.*]

He seems a little changed from the Tuesday. His stoop is a trifle more ingrained and he watches his hands as though their movements were outside his volition. They are taped at the ends to prevent blistering and present a curious club-like appearance as they stab at the tunes, a half-hit note thickening the texture of the playing.

[*The piano takes over playing in the manner indicated. The tune can be anything sweet and medium tempo. It fades out after a while for the* NARRATOR.]

All through the day he plays, watched by a steady trickle of women shoppers and children and casual passers-by, drawn in to see the man who has sat up all night at a piano. An admission can has been set up and they drop their sixpences and stand round.

[*A bridge piece with the piano playing 'I Can't Give You Anything But Love, Baby' and the staccato sound of coins being dropped into an empty can. There are a number of voices, two men, two women, and a child. They have a stylized, bodiless quality and should give if possible the impression of one composite mind thinking a montage of thoughts. The piano plays behind.*]

w: He looks awful tired, poor soul –
w: So he should too –
m: He'll be getting drugs to keep him going –
w: Can you play 'Night and Day'? –

[*This in a derisive way and draws some laughter. The piano is un-heeding.*]

c: Is he going to die, mummy?
w: No he's not going to die, he's just playing the piano.
m: They'll have him well drugged up with that benzedrine stuff –
w: I wonder when they will feed him, I'd like to watch him being fed –
w: How will he play when he's getting fed?

w: He's got to or he's disqualified –

m: You'd think all that drugging would give them a taste for it –

m: A lot of these musicians take drugs, you're always reading about it in the papers –

c: Mummy, what's wrong with him?

w: There's nothing wrong with him . . . he's just playing the piano –

c: What is it he's playing?

w: Can you play 'Night and Day' –

[*Laughter and fade leaving the piano to play a sad discordant passage on the chords of 'Night and Day'. The* NARRATOR *comes in.*]

He goes on through the day giving the piano no rest, smoking cigarettes as they are lit for him, smoking idly, blue sinews of smoke rising above his head, rarely looking at the spectators, going on timelessly, aimlessly, towards tomorrow.

[*Piano plays 'Time on My Hands' briefly.* NARRATOR.]

In the evening young people going to the dancing and the pictures look in at the strange hermit, chained by the hands to his cell; the girls with their bright lacquered faces look at the greying features of this eight-day ascetic and find his vocation disturbing and his music devoid of anything save duration.

[*The piano plays a bleak chorus of 'For Ever and Ever'.* NARRATOR.]

Occasionally the pianist talked to George his assistant.

[GEORGE'S *voice is young and commonplace and the* PIANIST *has the same long pauses before his lines. The piano plays throughout.* GEORGE *speaks first* . . .]

How do you feel?

Not too bad, a bit sore –

Do you want a cushion?

No, I'll stand up in a minute. Funny I feel I could go for a long walk and when I came back it would still be playing –

Just don't you try it –

No, no, I won't try it. It's against me this piano, it's not going to play itself. Sometimes it's like trying to push something, not like trying to play a piano at all, something heavy, it's like a weight. I get tired –

Of course you do –

Not just like that, not tired that way. Really tired. You know. Really tired in where you can't reach it. Tired –

Of course you do. Will I get you a cushion? –

No, I'll stand up in a minute. Light me a fag, will you –

[*The piano jogs on, a match is struck. The* PIANIST *is heard to inhale and exhale deeply like a sigh. Piano.* NARRATOR.]

Darkness falls and the streets empty and the room is left to the pianist and George, the manager and a judge. Occasionally a passing policeman looks in with official nosiness and chats to the manager and sees under the illumination of an adjustable lamp, two hands lurch and touch and at times stumble over one another, an unceasing courtship in which the protagonists have forgotten the meaning of the ritual.

[*The piano comes in and under its jangle the sound of the* PIANIST'S *heart and breathing can be heard, with stethoscopic intimacy, providing an accompaniment to the tuneless noise of the piano. The* NARRATOR *comes in, his voice soft and ruthful.*]

Half asleep and with no vestige of musical coherency, a tune fading out in a welter of wrong notes and half-hit chords, a music of derangement and fatigue, jangling on into the night, heard only by the late courters coupling in closes . . .

[*Mumbles and breathing of lovers. Piano . . .*]

. . . or foreign sailors singing in unison, songs of men far from warm homes . . .

[*Faintly men sing, sweet and indistinct. The piano rises to drown it. Holds.* NARRATOR . . .]

through the night he plays . . .

[*Piano in the pause . . .*]

. . . for no one save the unheeding cats . . .

[*Catcalls and piano duet for a moment . . .*]

. . . the adjacent insomniac . . .

[*Bedsprings move, indistinct sleepless mutter, ticking of a loud clock and the piano . . .*]

. . . and the metronomic policeman . . .

[*Footfalls and metronome, a steady regular beat against which the piano tries to keep time, fails and goes raggedly on while the other sounds fade . . .*]

. . . plays a pure idiot music, a carol of loneliness and futility.

[*The piano plays on and on. The sounds played above are run through again spaced out in the monotony of the piano and finally in a mix they are superimposed, the policeman walking through the dreams of the sleepless, the clock and the metronome, slightly out of time, the cats and the lovers and the fading sound of singing. The piano goes on after they have passed.* NARRATOR.]

The morning comes without haste, discolouring the east and diminishing the spotlight that illumines his hands, five-legged and bat blind. He is fed and washed, his shirt changed and fresh hot water bottles placed in his lap to diminish the cramps that seize him at that hour. So the first visitor finds him, the hours of pseudo-sleep behind him, awaiting the slow attrition of another day.

[*Piano plays a broken version of 'Time On My Hands'.*]

The manager chalks up on the board a trinity of Normals.

[*Sound of chalk squeaking and over it breathing and heartbeats, a little stertorous. Piano.* NARRATOR.]

He then goes outside to have a look at the morning.

[*A montage of morning sounds, brisk walking, bicycle bell, dog barks, Good mornings. The piano deciphers the code of 'Oh What A Beautiful Morning'.* NARRATOR.]

Across in the billiard saloon the two old men who look after the tables discuss the phenomenon.

[*They are two gnarled voices, dueting rather than conversing.*]

Playing on like that, it's daft, can't be good for you –

Can't be, must be a terrible strain on the nerves, must go for the nerves –

Must do, the nerves is a dangerous thing, it doesn't do to meddle with the nerves –

There was never anything like that in our day, a man playing a piano for a week –

Never, I can never remember the likes of it –

Do you remember the escaper that used to come?

A big fellow, great big fellow –

No he wasn't very big, about your size he was –

That's right, they tied him up in chains and a strait-jacket and threw him into the harbour –

And he was down for three minutes and they thought he was dead –

Then he came up with the chains –

About the size of me he was –

That's right. That big fellow you're talking about was the strong man –

That's right, he used to let you break stones on his chest with a hammer –

Strongest man I ever saw was old Harry the blacksmith, I saw him stop a coal cart one day when the horse bolted. All down the street it went, coal and sparks off its hooves everywhere and Harry ran out and . . . and caught it by the bridle and held it –

There's nobody like that nowadays –

Not at all, things are all different –

Who ever heard of a man playing a piano for a week –

Never, things aren't the same –

It just shows you how things have changed –

It's a sign of the times –

That's true enough, a sign of the times –

[*There is a pause and the piano can be heard, distant.*]

Mind you I suppose he'll be a good enough pianist –

Oh he'll be a good enough pianist all right –

[*Piano comes in again, faint then increasing in volume until the tune is heard – it is 'In the Good Old Summertime'. After a moment the* NARRATOR.]

Later in the day the local newspaper sent their reporter to cover the event. The manager took him into a back room and gave him the relevant details.

[*The* REPORTER *is an anonymous voice, asking questions. The piano is muffled. The* MANAGER *speaks first . . . his tone is professional and rehearsed.*]

This is a tremendous feat you understand, tremendous. It's reckoned by the medical profession that the strain involved in playing for so long is equal to the strain of climbing Mount Everest. That German, him that holds the world record just now, well he was in hospital for almost a month –

And do you think that will happen to your man?

No, I don't. You see we've approached this scientifically, we have planned a special diet and he's had special training –

Is this his first attempt at the record?

It's the first time he's tried it under my management. He tried it once before on his own –

And how long did he play for?

Sixty hours –

That's not very long compared with what he's got to play now –

That's true, but then he wasn't trained. He just sat down and played until he dropped, no system. It's different this time –

And what's the secret of your system?

Well I'm afraid that's something that I'm not at liberty to divulge. You see, I'm under contract to one of the big papers to sell the story along with the secret of my training methods –

And what sort of money does your man stand to gain if he beats the record?

Well there's no guarantee in this game, we might get a few television appearances and a few public shows; what we really want is a trip to the States to stage some public contests –

And what if your man doesn't make it?

We don't think like that. Just you go out there and have a look and you'll see he's still going strong –

[*A door opens and the piano fills the sound. The tune is 'I'm Sitting on Top of the World'.* NARRATOR.]

There were a number of visitors at dinner-time to see him being fed.

[*Sound of money being dropped in the tin. Piano. This goes on under the* NARRATOR'S *voice for a time.*]

Some girls giggled when George tied a bib under his chin. He was fed with a spoon and then his meat was cut up and he ate it from a fork. Afterwards he drank a bottle of milk through a straw and smoked a cigarette. All the while he played the piano and after a time it did not seem so strange that he should.

[*Piano plays here, sliding from a tune into a number of mournful chords on the left hand, with a blues feeling but no rhythmic impulse. These chords continue through the next narration.*]

Later in the evening it began to rain. It fell in long straight lances, freckling the windows and thickening the air.

[*At this point rain begins to creep into the sound as it slowly builds up in volume, the piano continues with its heavy solitary chords. The two sounds reach equality and go on for a moment longer; when the narration restarts the rain swells to become dominant.*]

It rains with a full limpid abandon, falling with swift simple fall in tender teemings of wet, germinant upon the streets into brief up-blossomings, wet petallations that flower and fade almost before the eye can taste them.

[*The rain sound has changed to the drumming of rain on canvas or metal. Not the noise of its fall but of its impact. It is faded sharply and the piano re-enters, the chords now right hand and dissonant and accelerating in their frequency towards some sort of climax. They persist behind the narration.*]

While the pianist in his desert strikes dry flakes from the keys until the dust rises and chokes him . . .

[*The piano is now sounding one flinty chord after another without respite. Gradually increasing in volume the rapid breathing and pounding heart of the* PIANIST. *Out of this millrace of sound comes his voice, choked and desperate and small . . .*]

Open the window!

[*A moment's silence, a window goes up and an immense wet volume of rain drowns the sound track. It holds for a moment until under it, subordinate but distinct, the narration.*]

And let the small rain down rain into this aridity of life without the moisture of meaning, down to the parched roots of this rooted to the ground growth, this poor plant, this long-distance piano-player of a musicless world.

[*The voice ends and after its compassion the piano plays on sadly amid the soft hiss of the rain. Later the* NARRATOR.]

The rain also brought in two drunk men who tried to detect the tune in progress, failed and began to protest.

[*The voices are stylized drunk. The piano tinkles on behind.*]

What's that you're playing; give us one of the old ones.

It's a recital –

Give us one of the old ones, play 'Ramona', that's an old one, play 'Ramona'.

[*He starts to sing 'Ramona'. The other drunk joins him. They sound drunk but they are in tune. The* MANAGER *interrupts them . . .*]

Gentlemen, I'm sorry but you can't sing in here, it's not for singing to.

Well, let's dance then.

No dancing, gentlemen, please, if you please, no dancing and no singing, it's not allowed.

What's it for then?

What's he playing for then? You can't dance and you can't sing . . .

And you can't make out the tunes. What's he playing for then . . .

Yes, tell us, what's he playing for?

[*Their voices fade and the piano rises in a little rash of exasperation up the scale then slackens for the* NARRATOR.]

The two men finally leave protesting a swindle and asking for money they did not pay to be refunded.

[*Indistinct protests and then the* NARRATOR *goes on.*]

They leave the group to another vigil, sustained by coffee and cigarettes while outside the windows of the town are extinguished and night is everywhere.

[*A series of night sounds; wind, the creaking of signs, a dustbin lid and the piano making a thin moan. The* NARRATOR *goes on.*]

The music of the piano has now pared itself down into a sequence of jagged sounds, which sift through the walls of near-by dwellings and are construed by the half-awake into a perpetually unfolding theme of unrecognizable familiarity, the climax of which remains in the future and fills the hearer with a frustration almost sweet in its faintness.

[*Piano played through baffles to attain the effect described leads through the above passage until the* NARRATOR *stops and it is heard alone. When the* NARRATOR *starts again there is heard very faintly a dance band playing in a dated style, 'Ramona'.*]

They listen to the fragile skein of song beside sleeping partners and unearth attic memories of themselves, slender and soft handed, with colour in their dresses and their faces, when worlds revolved on dance floors of desiring.

[*'Ramona' swells and fades and the piano is left thin and weak.*]

Above wet slums and steep slate, tinsel tinkling in the dreams of the town the notes rise until the steady sift of rain bedraggles them earthwards.

[*The piano fades very slowly. Then a synthetic sound, an amalgam of alarum-clock and cock-crowing, fading to allow the* NARRATOR.]

Clock-crow finds the world wan and wind-whipped. Chimneys churn and smoke from early morning fires is strung in long scarves above the roofs. Blown madly over the town like scraps of tissue the notes are scarcely heard and people have to look in to assure themselves that he is still playing. He sits with a waning will and ashen eyes, his hands like two drugged rodents in a cage, all but impervious to their constant collisions.

[*Piano and breathing and the violent thudding of the heart go on for a time then* GEORGE *and the* MANAGER *speak. The piano can be heard behind them erratic. The* MANAGER *speaks first.*]

He's looking a bit dicy this morning, George.

144

THE LONG-DISTANCE PIANO-PLAYER

I thought he was going to keel over last night just after you turned in, I couldn't get him to answer me and his hands kept falling off the piano –

You usually get that about the middle of the course, they're sure they can't go any further but you just have to talk them over it. Come on, we'll have a talk with him, this is where a manager really counts.

[*There is a pause during which the piano makes noises and the breathing and the heartbeats are heard. While the* MANAGER *is talking to the* PIANIST *this can be heard behind his voice and in the gaps when he pauses for a reply it is this sound that can be heard on the track.*]

How's it going? George says you were nearly away last night. [*Pause.*] Well, that's the worst of it over now. [*Pause.*] That's the back of it broken. [*Pause.*] Could be doing with a shave though. [*Pause.*] You'll feel better after a shave. Just you wait and see –

[*Piano and sounds go on for a time. The* NARRATOR *comes in, the piano behind.*]

The barber came just before dinner and they brought out a little card-table and he prepared his implements, the water hot and clean, steaming in a small enamel bowl, a fresh towel over his arm, the razor sharp and shining steel. He lathered the pianist's face carefully, standing behind him and rubbing in the soap. He lathered him a rich creamy white like childhood snow. The pianist let his head fall back and his throat was taut and exposed. He looked up at the barber's overhead, inverted face as he shaved him. The stubble yielded to the razor in a small keen crackling and he wiped the curds of soap on a piece of paper.

[*There follows the speech of the* PIANIST *which is punctuated by the comments of the* BARBER, *the sound of the razor and the piano rambling on. The sound of the razor should act as a simile of the* BARBER'S *remarks and the piano of course will parallel the broken soliloquy of the* PIANIST. *The* BARBER *speaks first.*]

Hold it steady now sir, that's it. [*Razor sound.*]

It's getting heavy to hold . . . heavy . . . getting heavy . . . too heavy . . . can't . . . heavy . . . oh it's heavy . . .

Just hold it a moment, sir. [*Razor.*]

Too heavy to push . . . tired . . . tired tired tired tired . . . getting very tired in the morning when you waken . . . waken from sleep . . . it's waiting . . . heavy –

That's it, sir, just a little, that's it – [*Razor.*]

You can't lift it it's so so so heavy . . . you're tired . . . so so so tired . . . a piano's heavy . . . very heavy every morning . . .

Over this way sir, fine. [*Razor.*]

It's there . . . your piano . . . get it up on your back . . . heave . . . the back of it is broken now it's so heavy . . . everybody has to pick it up . . . everybody so tired . . . pick up your piano and play . . . play . . . tired . . . cushion no good . . . so tired . . .

Now the other side. [*Razor.*]

You fall down . . . in the end you fall down . . . all fall down . . . it's so heavy . . . my back is broken now . . . give me a cushion . . .

Just a moment now, there we are, hold still now. [*Razor.*]

Always tired . . . piano . . . piano . . . pick it up . . . heavy heavy piano . . . push . . . carry . . . carry . . . push . . . all . . . all . . . all play piano . . . heavy . . .

There we are, sir, how does that feel?

Feels heavy . . . oh, it's heavy . . . very heavy . . . every morning it's waiting to be picked up . . . piano . . . piano . . . when it falls it makes a noise all the strings all the notes all at once and the noise is everywhere every note ever played it plays all the tunes you made me love you you are my sunshine night and day you always hurt the one you hear them all and every morning you pick them all up and you hear them all fall down . . .

[NARRATOR *comes in after a pause and as he speaks the piano is playing slowly and deep on the left hand.*]

He plays now with a calm heaviness, the notes ripe and perfumed, random as fruitfall in an autumn of inconsequence. In this twilight of sound the only spectator is an old woman with a shawl over her head. She has found a chair and sits with her hands crocheted on her lap and in her mind a summer moulders long and warm ago. The pianist looks at her and seems to see her and she smiles at him, a smile of age, wrinkling her face. So they watch each other and the music reaches down beyond tedium and sorrow to play bass and sabbath sounding a psalm of resignation.

[*Piano plays deep, heavy chords. Fade as* NARRATOR *comes in.*]

He does not see the old woman leave, he slips from moment to moment into a coma of fatigue and the streets are dark and in the wind rising before he is jolted awake by George with coffee.

Come on, drink this, there's rum in it, it'll do you good, drink it –

[*The* NARRATOR *takes up the final speech with the piano sounding more and more ominous as it goes on. Now there is concentrated in the piano a blind beaten rage which is counterbalanced by the compassion of the voice. It is a poem set to music.*]

He plays on into the uncaring night, thrashing his arms in minute convulsions over the limitless waste of the keyboard. There is now no idea left in his being of melody or theme, the bruised bunches of his fingers stub themselves bluntly and there rises into the night the authentic music of the world, a series of inarticulate cries without shape or intent, beyond hope of justification or understanding, a jangle of clotted vibrations that transcend discordancy and under the lunatic eye of the moon dwindle into silent slivers of spent sound.

[*The piano plays on, and on, and on.*]

END

CECIL P. TAYLOR

Happy Days are Here Again

Happy Days are Here Again was first broadcast in the
B.B.C. Third Programme on 20 January 1967 with
the following cast:

LIPHITZ	Roddy McMillan
WAXMAN	Walter Jackson
DONOVAN	David McKail
ANGEL	Harry Webster
POSTMAN	Henry Stamper
MONTY	Harry Walker
DETECTIVE	James Gavigan

Produced by Stewart Conn

Music: 'Happy Days are Here Again' which fades during the narration.

ANNOUNCER: It is an afternoon in winter. The living-room of Liphitz's house is a shambles. . . . Old newspapers and items of clothing litter the chairs and floor. At one corner of the room is an old, shabby couch. In the other, an old-fashioned acoustical gramophone. In the centre is a table, crammed with packages and jars of food, as if Liphitz has laid out his entire larder. Liphitz is sitting at the table, picking at the crumbs on the newspaper table-cloth. Waxman enters. He looks at Liphitz. Liphitz ignores him. Slowly, Waxman removes his overcoat. He looks towards Liphitz again, but getting no response, clears a pile of newspapers from the couch and sits.

[*A long pause.*]

WAXMAN [*suddenly*]: If everything goes all right, I'll take her to the mountains for a weekend.

LIPHITZ: Will you? That's a good idea. An excellent idea.

WAXMAN: I once hired a boat for a weekend one summer. And I kept sailing into the sun. I particularly enjoyed breakfasting on the beach when the sun just came up. The water was burning with it!

LIPHITZ: Why didn't you go with her to London?

WAXMAN: Liphitz! I've got my work. . . . I just can't take –

LIPHITZ: You're a prole, Waxman! You hear me? A prole!

WAXMAN: I sent my sister with her.

LIPHITZ: A coward, Waxman! You didn't like the idea of coming back with her coffin. That was it, wasn't it, Waxman?

WAXMAN: I know you, Liphitz!

LIPHITZ: It repelled you, didn't it, Waxman? The idea of going down with a lovely, living girl – and coming back with her coffin.

WAXMAN: I know you, Liphitz. You're just trying to frighten me. I know, Liphitz. . . . It's just a routine operation . . .

LIPHITZ: Donovan says it's highly dangerous. I said to Donovan 'Speaking as a scientist, Donovan, what do you think about this operation?' 'It's highly dangerous,' he said.

WAXMAN: Donovan thinks he knows everything! You're always bumming up Donovan to me!

LIPHITZ: Donovan will be here shortly. They're all coming. . . . I'm having a little party . . . for all her friends . . .

WAXMAN [*savagely*]: You and her fancy, intellectual friends! Bugger them!

   [*Pause.* WAXMAN *produces a bag of raisins.*]

   I've brought you some raisins, Liphitz . . .

   [LIPHITZ *grabs them and begins eating, greedily . . . but continues to ignore* WAXMAN.]

   You didn't tell me you were thinking of throwing a party, Liphitz . . .

   [LIPHITZ *continues to ignore him.*]

   Are they all coming? All those intellectuals?

LIPHITZ: Waxman. Consider the tragedy. All those fine men, men of worth, men of wisdom, leaders by virtue of their knowledge. She has slept with them all. And she gets a child by you! Weak, puny-minded, muddled, dripping wet Waxman!

WAXMAN: Can I have a raisin, Liphitz?

LIPHITZ [*standing up and looking at him in disgust*]: Nothing but body! Big, massive, butcher body!

WAXMAN: Liphitz, I want you to listen to me. . . . Please, Liphitz . . . I love Ruth. . . . I assure you, Liphitz. . . . I do . . .

LIPHITZ: That is not true, Waxman.

WAXMAN: I do, Liphitz. . . . I assure. . . . I love –

LIPHITZ: That is not true, Waxman! Otherwise you could never have seduced her. Otherwise, having seduced her, you would never have gotten her with child. Otherwise, having gotten her with child, you would never have sent her to London to procure an abortion. Otherwise! Otherwise! An infinity of otherwises! These are very fine raisins, Waxman.

   [*Pause.*]

WAXMAN: When do you think we'll get a phone call, Liphitz?

LIPHITZ: Yes! All those fine intellectuals will be coming. Postman, Donovan, Angel . . . Monty. . . . They'll all be here. . . . You will be able to appreciate your natural inferiority to the fullest depth. . . . Your total, prole, conformist, sleepwalking inadequacy, Waxman!

WAXMAN [*suddenly – to disprove him*]: I read a book last week. . . . That Ruth gave me. . . . On biochemistry. . . . Simplified, I admit . . . but deep and hard reading. . . . I read it . . . I finished it. . . . Right to the very end! I know all about the chemistry of life now. . . . You hear that. . . ? I can analyse you, Liphitz! I can. You hear that? I can analyse man. You take a pail. . . . You put in some carbon, hydrogen, nitrogen –

LIPHITZ: I will get you a pail, Waxman.

WAXMAN: Liphitz, I don't need a pail. . . . I was just using the pail . . . to . . . you know what . . . to illustrate my point . . .

LIPHITZ: Waxman! I will get you a pail!

WAXMAN: You add some sulphur . . . sodium . . . potassium . . .

LIPHITZ [*approaches*]: I regret I have no pail, Waxman. But this basin should do very well.

WAXMAN: Liphitz, I don't need a basin . . . I've finished what I had to say . . . I don't need it.

LIPHITZ: But the basin is obviously required. The basin is here. Therefore, Waxman, it is required. Conversely, if it were not here, it would not be required. Let us not split hairs, Waxman. Surely this obvious fact must penetrate even your puny, dull, opaque, foggy intellect . . .

WAXMAN [*in a fury*]: Liphitz, I don't question anything! Nothing, Liphitz! I'm bloody sick of you!

LIPHITZ: Where did you buy such fine raisins, Waxman? Buy me some more. A large quantity in future. . . . The bag's finished. . . .

WAXMAN: Everybody is sick of you, Liphitz! Ruth is sick of you. . . . Your intellectual headaches are sick of you. . . . Somebody wants to make a recording of you and play it back to you. . . . You would be sick of you!

[LIPHITZ *returns to the table, cuts himself a thick slice of bread.* WAXMAN *cools down. . . . He watches* LIPHITZ *eating, enviously . . .*]

Could I have some bread, Liphitz?

LIPHITZ [*cutting him a slice – generously*]: Here, Waxman. Eat. . . . Take salt. . . . Take pepper. . . .

[WAXMAN *comes to the table.*]

What are you looking for, Waxman?

WAXMAN: Margarine.

LIPHITZ: Stop it! Will you! Stop disarranging my table! If you must have margarine with your new-found biochemical knowledge, synthesize yourself some! [*He laughs himself into hysterics over his joke.*]

WAXMAN [*eating*]: It will do very well as it is, Liphitz. It's very tasty. . . . Liphitz, when will the others be coming?

LIPHITZ: You are afraid. You are about to feel your smallness, your weakness . . . to the bone. . . . Do not be afraid, Waxman. You are what you are. . . . And I will be with you. I will be with you, Waxman.

WAXMAN: You're trying to make me feel small again, aren't you, Liphitz? But I know myself, Liphitz. I'm sure of myself. I'm an engineer!

LIPHITZ: I will stay with you all the time. I will be your anchorage in the storm of your inferiority, Waxman.

WAXMAN [*boasting*]: I create with my hands, Liphitz. I'm the tide, Liphitz. You can't keep back the tide. I am the masses, Liphitz. . . . I am the majority. We've already taken over one-third of the world. You'll have to make way for me one of these days – All of you . . . Liphitz! I am the future!

LIPHITZ [*standing up – shouting over* WAXMAN]: Don't shout, Waxman! Do you hear me! Don't shout! Is it simply impossible for you to maintain a logical conversation? [*Raging.*] Shouting, banging, raging, raping. . . . Fill the world with ugliness and noise! [*His rage subsides.*] – You must not be offended when I rebuke you, Waxman. I am attempting to instruct you. There is simply no reason for shouting. A total waste of energy. Nobody listens to shouting. . . .

WAXMAN: They listened to Hitler.

LIPHITZ [*going over to the window*]: No. They did not listen to Hitler. Hitler was not listened to. He shouted. He raged – and was not listened to – Not . . . listened . . . to . . . remotely . . . partially.

WAXMAN: He was impotent, Hitler. . . . You know that?

LIPHITZ [*now at the gramophone*]: I will now play you a little music. We have only the slow movement of The Unfinished . . . and it sticks just where the oboe comes in. Nevertheless, I personally find it very narcotic . . . very soothing. . . . Fenderman next door's going out.

WAXMAN: To hell with Fenderman!

LIPHITZ: He's got his best suit on. The blue and grey one.

WAXMAN [*with sudden decision*]: Look . . . Liphitz, what's the number? I'm going to phone the doctor.

LIPHITZ: You think he's going out with a girl? In that case it's going to be a long business. Quite possibly Fenderman will be away all night.

WAXMAN: Please, Liphitz. . . . What's the doctor's number?

LIPHITZ: I don't know, Waxman, how should I know the doctor's
number?

WAXMAN: What's his name? We can get the number from Directory.

LIPHITZ: He had a very fine name. A ringing name. It stood out.
Monty told me. . . . Incidentally, when you see Monty – you must
thank him for what he's doing. I told you Monty would pay – I
told him about Ruth. . . . He said, 'Don't worry . . . I've got a good
man in London to look after that little job.'

WAXMAN: Liphitz, what's his name?

LIPHITZ: As I say, it stood out . . . Harrison? Or Gersoovitch? No.
Wait a minute. Doberman. Binderman. The best thing to do is to
wait for Monty. Monty'll tell you in a minute.

WAXMAN [lifting the telephone]: We'll try Binderman.

LIPHITZ: You think that might be the name? Quite possibly. Very
possibly.

WAXMAN [dials repeatedly with no result]: What's happened to your
telephone, Liphitz?

LIPHITZ: The telephone is cut off, Waxman.

[WAXMAN crashes the receiver down in anger.]

It's been cut off for weeks. It's much better now. I like it exactly like
this. I can telephone who I like . . . anywhere in the world –
absolutely free! With not one side effect. [Lifts receiver.] Hullo –
Epstein? This is Liphitz! You're a swine! A bastard! A fascist!
You'd be better dead! [To WAXMAN.] Or sometimes, when lust
suddenly seizes my declining body. [Into telephone.] Miriam darling
– Liphitz here, my dove – Listen, my lovely, sweet girl – my whole
body's broken out in a rash of love. Hurry up and come over. . . .
Bring wine . . . will you? Sherry . . . [Replacing the receiver.] You
see, Waxman? Not one side effect, whatsoever! And absolutely free
of charge!

WAXMAN [desperately]: Liphitz, tell me this. How are we going to get
a message from Ruth?

LIPHITZ: I told you. They're all coming round to hear what happened. Naturally, they're anxious to find out the result of this
highly dangerous, hazardous operation. They want to meet you,
too. . . . The telephone is irrelevant, Waxman. Use your puny
mind! They're going to ring to Fenderman's. . . . Next door.

WAXMAN: Fenderman's gone out.

LIPHITZ: His mother is in.

WAXMAN: Fenderman has a mother?

LIPHITZ: They live together. His mother's stone deaf. Gets on his nerves – He's admitted it to me. In confidence, you understand, Waxman. That's why he has to go out to have his girls.

WAXMAN: Fenderman's mother's stone deaf?

LIPHITZ: Can't hear a thing. Fenderman says it's the nerve-centres. It's psychosomatic. She had a bad marriage. When she washes her hair she can hear for ten minutes after. You want to analyse Fenderman's mother with your new-found physiological knowledge, Waxman? Oh, you're worried about how she's going to hear the phone? She can't hear the phone, naturally – she's stone deaf.

WAXMAN: Fenderman's out for the night. And Fenderman's mother's stone deaf.

LIPHITZ: Can't hear a thing! But they have a little light in the kitchen. When the phone rings, the light flashes. Most scientific. Speaking as a scientist what do you think of this, Waxman?

WAXMAN: I think I'm sick.

LIPHITZ [*continuing his story*]: So the little light flashes. Should Fenderman be out, as is the case at the present time, the mother goes to the phone . . . and says . . . 'I'm sorry – I'm stone deaf. But my son will be in at such and such a time – please ring back then.' A very scientific well-thought arrangement, don't you think, Waxman? You wouldn't think Fenderman would have it in him! Anyway, tonight, they are waiting for a phone call from Ruth . . . in London . . . for me. . . . So Fenderman has given his mother a big stick. . . . Every time the phone rings, she goes to it, says, 'I'm stone deaf, but please hold on one minute.' She knocks on the adjoining wall to this . . . and I go to answer it.

WAXMAN [*relieved*]: Oh – that's fine. . . . You have an arrangement with them.

LIPHITZ: I just keep going back and forwards until Ruth . . . or your sister . . . or the doctor . . . comes on.

[POSTMAN *enters.*]

Here's Postman! Good! Excellent! I hope he's brought his poems. He's the very first. We don't count you, Waxman.

[POSTMAN *is carrying a stick of salami in one hand – and a manuscript in the other. He stares at Waxman.*]

That's him, Postman! That's Waxman!

POSTMAN: Nothing much to look at, is he?

LIPHITZ: Got a good body.

POSTMAN: Plenty of him. But what about quality?

LIPHITZ: Intellect, puny, I'm sorry to say, Postman. Exceedingly puny!

POSTMAN: You can see that. All body. Any phone call about Ruth yet, Liphitz?

WAXMAN: What's that to you?

LIPHITZ: Fenderman's gone out to a girl. But as yet, no phone call from London, Postman. Very likely, there are complications. Donovan said, 'There is every likelihood of complications.'

POSTMAN [*still ignoring* WAXMAN]: Unnecessary business in the first place. A bit of common sense and she wouldn't have needed any operation. Look how many of us have loved her – Look how many have patronized her in her line of business – And never any bother like that.

LIPHITZ: Exactly! Till Waxman turns up! Did you bring your poems?

POSTMAN: I have them here.

LIPHITZ: You'll read them, of course, during the proceedings.

POSTMAN: Will he understand them?

WAXMAN: I don't understand you!

LIPHITZ: There's nothing to understand about Postman. He's a poet. He came here one day to deliver a parcel to Ruth and ended up in her bed.

POSTMAN: I was very much in love with her.

WAXMAN [*sarcastically*]: And she with you.

POSTMAN [*to* WAXMAN]: Naturally. And still is.

LIPHITZ: This is for me, Postman? That's nice. Salami – how thoughtful of you, Postman. [*Smelling it, changing his tone.*] I thought so! That's just like you! You can never do anything right! It's without garlic!

POSTMAN: I'm sorry, Liphitz – I am.

LIPHITZ: You know my views on salami without garlic. It has no taste without.

WAXMAN: I've noticed that.

LIPHITZ: Salt without pepper – a ship without a rudder.

POSTMAN: I'm very sorry, Liphitz – I thought – seeing they were all coming, it would be safer.

LIPHITZ: That's right! That's why you never get anywhere! Play safe. Play safe all the time! In your work. In your poetry – In your attitude to life. This is you, Postman. Salami without garlic! Where did you get it from?

POSTMAN: In a little delicatessen shop – just at the corner.

LIPHITZ: Go back and change it. For one with garlic – and get a full stick – Don't be stingy – I'm expecting friends – you know that! [POSTMAN *is about to go.*] Leave your poems here. . . . Wait a minute. [*He pulls the salami from his hand and cuts a slice.*]

POSTMAN [*protesting*]: Liphitz – they won't . . .

LIPHITZ: They'll never miss a small slice – go on – hurry up.

    [POSTMAN *goes out.* LIPHITZ *takes the manuscript.*]

I'll read you some of his poems. This salami . . . No taste – whatsoever.

WAXMAN: Liphitz – do Ruth and Postman still . . .

LIPHITZ [*turning over the pages of the manuscript*]: Here's a good one!

> To cite a case,
> One of those literary chaps,
> For whom love, birth and death
> Are just strong copy for a poem.
>
> He had himself a dream when he was young.
> He dreamt he gathered in the points of time,
> Which linked and meshed him with the whole –
> And weaved from them a timeless web.

WAXMAN: Did he write that crap?

LIPHITZ [*continuing to read*]:

> He was quite committed after that!
> He hid himself in the Second Womb.
> Cocooned with pens and dictionaries.
> Outside were sores and lavatory walls,
> Inside – a meadow of April larks.

WAXMAN: Liphitz, what's it all about?

LIPHITZ: It's there – in the title.

WAXMAN [*reading*]: 'For Ruth'. Where does Ruth come in?

LIPHITZ: Let me finish, will you! Stop interrupting me . . . you're making me lose all the passion.

WAXMAN: All the passion! I want to know where the hell Ruth comes in there?

LIPHITZ: Here is Ruth. Listen closely, Waxman – Enter Ruth –

> He was a man with a grass beard
> And the copy fairly mounting for the poem,
> When he took out a new recording journal
> And wrote upon the title page: 'Love.'
>
> And Behold!
> The poem was a toy!
> A half-remembered childhood game
> And they were dunging the meadow of April larks
> Against the spring ploughing.

[POSTMAN *returns*. LIPHITZ *grabs the salami – cuts himself a slice – and eats.*]

Ah, Postman – Much better.

POSTMAN [*looking in the direction of the manuscripts*]: Well?

LIPHITZ: Would you like some bread, Postman?

POSTMAN: I'll wait for the others.

WAXMAN [*to* POSTMAN]: Are those poems any good you write?

POSTMAN: I hope so. . . . What do you think, Liphitz?

LIPHITZ: Personally, I'm not interested in poetry. If you've something to say, out with it. . . . What's the point in racking your brain for days on end for the smartest, prettiest, most obscure manner in which to say something?

WAXMAN: I once read something in the *Daily Worker* – It said 'Poetry is the distillation of the truth.' I think that's very true.

LIPHITZ: I did write one poem – many years ago – an excellent poem – a brilliant poem – it so dazzled me, I could not go on and write any more! It was so brilliant, so perfect a distillation of the truth, as our friend Waxman puts it, that anything else that followed would be certainly a pale shadow of my first-born. . . . I will recite it for you.

> Lord, in the beginning you were trying out your hand,
> When you laid out the seas and you laid out the land.
> You'd never created an earth like this before –
> Lord, I wished you'd've waited and practised some more!

WAXMAN [*impressed*]: Liphitz, did you really write that?

LIPHITZ: Well, Postman? I wouldn't give all your poems for my one masterpiece.

WAXMAN: What do you think of it, Postman? [*As he is speaking there is a dull, insistent knocking at the wall.*]

POSTMAN: It's clever. . . . I give you that. . . . Clever. . . . but . . .

WAXMAN [*to* LIPHITZ]: She's knocking . . .

LIPHITZ: What about the wonderful precision of language . . .

POSTMAN: The brilliant idea. . . ?

WAXMAN: Liphitz, she's knocking.

LIPHITZ: Who's knocking?

WAXMAN: The old woman. It must be Ruth.

LIPHITZ [*listening*]: Yes. . . . She is. . . . Kick the wall, will you, Waxman – while I get my coat and boots on.

WAXMAN [*kicking*]: Hurry up, Liphitz. She'll hang up!

LIPHITZ [*lacing his boots*]: I wouldn't bother kicking, Waxman. She can't hear you anyway. Come and help me on with my coat. [LIPHITZ *goes out.*]

POSTMAN [*taking up the manuscript*]: Do you want to hear some more?

WAXMAN: Yes. Read me some more. That's one thing I want to be able to understand – poetry. They appreciate poetry in the Soviet Union . . . ordinary people – they read Shakespeare, and buy poetry books. Some of the best-sellers in Russia are books of poetry.

POSTMAN: Listen to this:

> A man came to a man
> And said, 'teach me the Law'.
> And the man stood on a crutch of ice.
> And the sun burnt down on the earth
> And the man's clothes shrivelled to dust.
> And the flesh parted from his bones.
> But the crutch of ice was diamond-hard.
> And the man said – 'This is the Law!'

WAXMAN: Yes – I like that – but at the same time, it's hard to grasp . . . isn't it. . . . What was the one called 'Ruth' about?

POSTMAN: She might die, mightn't she? You keep hearing about these illegal operations – dirty instruments – blood poisoning.

WAXMAN: She won't die – that's just Liphitz trying to scare every-body.

POSTMAN: Every day you read about these things in the papers.

WAXMAN: She won't die! Monty's sent her to this doctor. . . . He's charging him through the nose – best man in the game! I'm telling you – she won't die . . .

[LIPHITZ *returns, as he is speaking. He takes off his coat and boots.*]
Well? [*impatiently*] Liphitz, is she all right?

LIPHITZ: The old woman is fine – excellent – exhausted, somewhat, after hammering at the wall, but this is only natural. . . . I told her this myself. . . . I said, it's only natural. . . .

WAXMAN: Liphitz – what about Ruth?

LIPHITZ: That wasn't Ruth. It was someone looking for the Civil Defence.

POSTMAN: Ah. . . . The Civil Defence.

LIPHITZ: I wonder if Fenderman is in the Civil Defence? He never mentioned anything to me about it. It might have been a wrong number. . . . Oh . . . Donovan will be here shortly. . . . I just met him coming along the road . . . and sent him off for something for our party. I said 'You must mean the undertakers . . .' 'No,' they said, 'the Civil Defence.' 'That's right, the undertakers . . .' 'Is this the Civil Defence?' they said. 'No,' I said, 'this is the Arctic Banana Plantation.' They rang off.

[DONOVAN *enters.*]
What did you buy, Donovan?

DONOVAN [*displaying a packet of cornflakes*]: This has everything, Lippy! Look here! Niacin . . . Vitamin B.1 . . . Vitamin B.2! Riboflavin! Cornflakes!

LIPHITZ [*taking the packet*]: Has it got a whistle in it? I'd like to have a whistle – I find them – entertaining.

DONOVAN [*studying the packet*]: Got a cut-out Space Ship.

LIPHITZ [*disappointed*]: A cut-out Space Ship!

DONOVAN: I'm not taking it back for one with a whistle, if that's what you're thinking about, Lippy.

LIPHITZ: I wasn't thinking of that.

DONOVAN: Yes you were. I know you, Lippy!

POSTMAN [*to* DONOVAN]: He sent me back to change the salami.

DONOVAN [*to* POSTMAN]: You bring some without garlic?

POSTMAN: Yes.

DONOVAN: You shouldn't have taken it back. His breath's poisonous enough as it is, without garlic!

LIPHITZ: Donovan, you're a swine! You hear me! A nonentity! A mass! A –

DONOVAN [*stretching out his hand for the salami*]: Come on, Lippy – let's have a slice.

LIPHITZ: I'm keeping it till everybody turns up.

DONOVAN: Lippy! Come on – give out with it –

LIPHITZ [*cutting a wafer-thin slice*]: Just a small slice –

DONOVAN [*grabbing it and turning to Waxman*]: You're Waxman?

WAXMAN [*hostile*]: That's right.

DONOVAN: What happened to you? Do you not know how to use contraceptives?

LIPHITZ [*delighted*]: I thought you'd bring that up, Donovan. That's the scientist in you.

DONOVAN [*to* WAXMAN]: They're cheap enough – aren't they?

WAXMAN [*embarrassed*]: What's it to you?

DONOVAN [*to* WAXMAN]: You're an up-to-date boy?

LIPHITZ [*to* DONOVAN]: An engineer. He is the future, Donovan.

DONOVAN [*to* WAXMAN]: You know the facts of life. Got to keep the old sperm from the egg – otherwise trouble!

LIPHITZ: He's studying science, too, Donovan.

DONOVAN: Bit late in the day, isn't it? Any message from London, yet?

POSTMAN: No – not yet.

LIPHITZ [*to* WAXMAN]: He's a fine fellow, Donovan, isn't he? He was gathering statistics on prostitution from Ruth . . . and he ended up in her bed . . .

DONOVAN: But I paid her well, Lippy. Spent half my grant on her! No money left to buy my books . . . that first year. . . . But she was an education. Waxman, did you find Ruth an education?

LIPHITZ [*to* DONOVAN]: Waxman is deeply in love with Ruth.

DONOVAN: So are we all. Does he pay her well? That's the question.

LIPHITZ [*with sarcasm*]: Donovan! How can you drag money into a question of deep love?

WAXMAN: Exactly!

LIPHITZ: Waxman drools over her – worships her – don't you, Waxman?

WAXMAN: Shut up, Liphitz!

DONOVAN: But pays her no money!

POSTMAN: Gets her into expense, more like it!

LIPHITZ: With all his heart and all his soul and all his might, our Waxman loves Ruth.

DONOVAN: And gets her with a kid!

POSTMAN: That's the thanks she gets!

DONOVAN: Queer way of showing love!

LIPHITZ [*taking up* POSTMAN'S *manuscript*]: Donovan, Postman has brought his poems. Will that be sufficient entertainment, do you think?

DONOVAN [*to* POSTMAN]: You brought your poems?

LIPHITZ [*to* DONOVAN]: He writes poems. Donovan, can you imagine anyone writing poems?

DONOVAN: I bet they're bloody wet poems – aren't they?

LIPHITZ: Donovan, they're wringing. [*Lifts the manuscript up.*] Moisture is oozing out of them!

DONOVAN [*looking at them*]: Tears?

LIPHITZ: And blood.

DONOVAN: Oh – blood.

LIPHITZ: Tears, naturally, too.

POSTMAN [*affronted*]: Some of my poems have been published.

LIPHITZ [*to* DONOVAN]: You hear that, Postman is recognized!

DONOVAN [*taking up the manuscript*]: Which are the dirty ones? I'll read them out.

LIPHITZ: That's right, Donovan – read us a poem.

DONOVAN: I'll do better – I'll make you one up.

LIPHITZ: Oh, fine, Donovan. . . . Very fine.

DONOVAN: Give me a subject.

LIPHITZ: Proles, Donovan.

DONOVAN: Proles and proud of it!
 Especially on Friday night,
 When the last hooter sounds,
 And we're beerward and whoreward !
 We think of the Industrial Revolution
 And the nature of the universe.

WAXMAN [*affronted*]: You think that's funny, Donovan! There's a reckoning coming – soon –

[*The old woman begins to knock on the wall again.*]

LIPHITZ: Beautiful, Donovan! Distilled truth! I see the stars before me, Donovan. I see the sun. The galaxies. [*He sits down at the table and opens the cornflake packet.*]

WAXMAN: Liphitz, she's knocking again.

LIPHITZ: Just when I was going to have some cornflakes.

POSTMAN: I'll go, Liphitz.

WAXMAN: I'll go.

LIPHITZ [*rising – shouting*]: Will you all keep quiet! I am going. She is my niece. Where's my coat?

WAXMAN: It's only next door, Liphitz!

LIPHITZ: Where's my boots? People come wandering into my house – disarranging everything – ruining all order – all routine – disintegrating my entire life.

WAXMAN: There's your boots.

LIPHITZ [*puts boots on and stands up*]: Please. I do not wish anybody to touch anything on the table, until I return. When I come back, we can eat.

WAXMAN: Liphitz, hurry up! She'll hang up! Please, Liphitz.

LIPHITZ [*going*]: I will give her all your love.

DONOVAN: Why can't Ruth phone here?

WAXMAN: It's cut off. There's a telephone next door.

POSTMAN: Chap by the name of Fenderman.

WAXMAN: His mother's the only one left in the house. Stone deaf ...
   [*Knock. Door opens.* ANGEL *enters. He coughs.*]

DONOVAN: Liphitz is next door, just now, Angel. Come in and join the company.

POSTMAN: Yes, we're a nice crowd here – all friends of the deceased.

ANGEL: Deceased?

POSTMAN: Don't listen to Donovan, Angel – there hasn't been any news yet.

DONOVAN: She might well be deceased by now. I keep telling you, those illegal operations are bloody risky! Thanks to our friend here, we might all be walking behind our best girl's coffin tomorrow!

ANGEL [*looking at* WAXMAN]: This is the man?

DONOVAN: This is Waxman. The lad she knew so potently! And this is Angel, the lusty lecher! Went round one morning to save Ruth and ended up in the same, characteristic situation as us all ...

POSTMAN: Donovan, you're a very coarse man!

ANGEL: And that isn't strictly correct – I admit, brothers, I did fall.

POSTMAN: Fall? Fall! That's blasphemy when you talk about relationships with Ruth!

ANGEL [*to* WAXMAN]: I understand your feelings well. I can feel the pain and grief in your heart. As I said, I, too, fell.

POSTMAN: And not just once, either, I bet!

DONOVAN: The falling would be a necessary stage in your religious development, Angel?

ANGEL: A stage, certainly.

DONOVAN: It gave you the feeling, eh? You came to know what it was to be a great sinner and succumb to the Flesh – to be caught in the web of lust?

POSTMAN: Where did you get all the vocabulary from, Donovan?

DONOVAN: From Angel, here. Been working on me for years.

ANGEL: I will only say this: the relationship between Ruth and I is now as father and daughter.

DONOVAN: Hear that, Waxie! You've got a new father-in-law.

ANGEL: Our love is beyond the Flesh.

POSTMAN: At the age of eighty-five, the rake enters a monastery.

DONOVAN: Anybody want to hear a good sermon?

ANGEL [*in a panic*]: Please. Give me those back. Those are private papers.

DONOVAN: Hey! Look at these, Postman. The Shipwrecked Sailor Saved. How the Word came to Peking. One million Bibles smuggled into Moscow. Here! What's this!

ANGEL: Please. . . . Let me have this back. . . . You wouldn't understand.

DONOVAN [*turning the pages*]: Oh, I understand all right, Angel. Very nice! Here! Look at this one, Postman.

[LIPHITZ *returns.*]

LIPHITZ: Oh, you've turned up at last, Angel. What have you brought me?

DONOVAN: He's brought you some nice pictures of girls.

POSTMAN: In various states of undress.

LIPHITZ: Angel, I specifically asked you to bring me something to eat – I'm having company.

WAXMAN: Was it Ruth?

LIPHITZ [*to* WAXMAN]: Will you stop bothering me just now! I am speaking to Angel! [*To* ANGEL.] I asked you, please, bring eatables – or drink. I wouldn't have objected to wine or spirits – but you bring me a pornographic book.

ANGEL: I didn't bring it for you. And it is by no means a pornographic book. It is a collection of photographic studies.

DONOVAN: Of the Flesh.

ANGEL: You see, Liphitz. It says on the front 'For the guidance of amateur photographers'. I am very interested in photography.

LIPHITZ: I would like a cine camera. Have you one? I would like to make a film of my day. From the minute I rise in the morning. Speaking as a photographic expert, Angel, would this be possible?

WAXMAN: Liphitz, what's happened to Ruth?

LIPHITZ: It wasn't Ruth. It wasn't a phone call at all. Fenderman's mother wished me to fill her hot-water bottle for her. As well as being stone-deaf, her eyesight is not what it should be [*taking off his things*]. She has double vision – I should imagine a complaint like that could be –

WAXMAN: Why don't you leave your coat on? There'll be a phone call any minute now.

LIPHITZ: The old woman asked a very deep question. She said, 'Mr Liphitz, why can't they make food out of coal? They make everything else out of coal. Why not food?' What do you think, Donovan?

DONOVAN: Let's eat, Liphitz. I'm hungry.

LIPHITZ: Coal has carbon in it. All food has carbon. You understand? I am giving you the basis of my argument. Why can't we extract food from coal? It would mean a new lease of life for coalmining. [*To* WAXMAN.] Waxman, speaking as a biochemist, what is your opinion?

DONOVAN: How about eating, Lippy?

LIPHITZ [*looking at* ANGEL]: Angel has brought nothing.

ANGEL [*producing a bag of apples*]: I have, Liphitz. . . . Here . . .

LIPHITZ [*emptying the bag on to the table*]: Yes – we need fruit. [*Counting*] Only five, Angel!

ANGEL: I'm sorry, Liphitz – I thought –

LIPHITZ: There's myself – Donovan, Monty, Postman, Angel and Waxman. Six, Angel!

ANGEL: Monty won't come. Those businessmen lead a very busy life.

LIPHITZ: Of course Monty will come. You will have to do without an apple.

ANGEL: Liphitz, if he was coming he'd be here by now.

LIPHITZ: Don't make excuses for your meanness, Angel. Monty is coming!

WAXMAN [*shouting*]: This is getting me down!

POSTMAN: Nothing can get you down.

DONOVAN: You can't sink any lower.

ANGEL: Charity, please. Exercise some human charity. . . . Love. . . .
Humanity . . .

LIPHITZ [to DONOVAN, POSTMAN and ANGEL]: You're just envious,
all of you, that Waxman has proved his virility with my niece.
Monty admitted as much to me, the other day.

DONOVAN: Liphitz, how did Monty take up with her. . . ?

LIPHITZ: She was out on Angel Street one night – exercising her
profession.

DONOVAN: Oh. She was out on the game!

LIPHITZ: He was extremely taken with her.

DONOVAN: No wonder! She's a lovely, succulent girl!

POSTMAN: She smells of peaches – of an orchard in spring.

DONOVAN: Yes! She's a beautiful, vital, lovely whore!

WAXMAN [seething with frustration]: This is getting me down.

ANGEL [going over to WAXMAN]: What is troubling you, Waxman?
Are the stresses and strains of waiting, telling on you? I understand
how you feel – I am sensitive to other men's sufferings – I feel it as
acutely –

WAXMAN: It's those disappearances of Liphitz. Every minute he goes
out next door. . . . You don't know what's happening. Whether it's
Ruth – or that – sod of a woman!

LIPHITZ [as if in reply, assuring WAXMAN]: You wait till you see what
Monty brings me! He'll bring wagonloads of goods. Like an
Eastern potentate! Whole chickens . . . smoked salmons . . .

DONOVAN: Shut up a minute, Lippy! You not see Waxman's
wilting?

[They all gather round him.]

LIPHITZ: So he is – he is pale – wilting, weak, witless Waxman.

WAXMAN: I'm all right – leave me alone, will you!

DONOVAN: It's bound to get on his nerves. . . . Lippy's performance.
The woman banging away at the wall – Lippy turning the room
upside down for his gear. Must you put on all your clobber when
you go to answer the phone, Lippy?

LIPHITZ: It's very cold, outside. It's necessary for me to be fully
clothed when I go out. You want me to wilt like Waxman? You
want me to get an infection –

DONOVAN: Dry up a minute, will you, Lippy! Let's get down to
applying the scientific method. We have a telephone . . .

LIPHITZ: It's a very fine telephone. Would you rather it was red?

ANGEL: I like a telephone in ivory.

POSTMAN: Virginal.

ANGEL: Ivory isn't virginal . . . white is . . . not ivory . . .

DONOVAN: Next door there is a line, connecting up Fenderman's telephone . . .

LIPHITZ: Fenderman's telephone is in splendid working order. I spoke to somebody before . . . looking for the Civil Defence . . . I said –

DONOVAN: I'll tell you what we're going to do! Take off the line from Fenderman's phone and connect it up to ours. That'll put us in communication with the outside world.

LIPHITZ: Yes . . . I would like being in communication with the outside world. . . . It would be something new for me. . . . It would be a real holiday. . . . Donovan, do this thing for me . . . please . . .

DONOVAN: Well now, Lippy, it's not quite as easy as all that . . .

LIPHITZ: Donovan, put me into communication with the outside world. . . . What are you waiting for?

DONOVAN: Lippy, it's not my branch. I'm a biologist. . . . I know the theory well enough . . .

LIPHITZ: That's exactly like you, Donovan! Talk . . . all talk. . . . Donovan knows everything. . . . But when it comes to action . . .

DONOVAN: I'm a biologist, Lippy!

LIPHITZ: Postman, you're in the communication business . . . you write poems . . .

POSTMAN: Liphitz, I can't. . . . I'm frightened of electricity. . . . It's . . .

ANGEL: I only wish I could help, Liphitz. . . . But I have no skill with my hands . . .

LIPHITZ: That's right. Run away from all your responsibilities! Go on! Cut me off from the outside world. . . . I know one thing. . . . Monty will do it for me when he comes . . .

DONOVAN: Don't talk wet, Lippy! What does Monty know about telephones?

[*While they are talking,* WAXMAN *has recovered. He rises.*]

WAXMAN [*trying to be casual . . . to suppress his pride*]: I could do it. . . . If I wanted to . . .

[*They all turn to him surprised.*]

LIPHITZ: Of course! Waxman is proficient in those matters. He is a wireman.

WAXMAN: An electrical engineer.

LIPHITZ: A very fine electrician! Look at his hands. . . . Fine strong hands. . . . Hands of the future. . . . Creative hands . . .

DONOVAN: If you need any help Waxman. I'm willing to –

WAXMAN: I'm not going to do it.

[*They stare at him.*]

That's final! I've been trodden on enough by you rotten, bourge bastards! All right. . . . Now we'll see where you'll get to with all your intellectual talk and fancy ideas and all the books you read . . .

DONOVAN: Now, look here, Waxman. . . . You're over-simplifying the whole situation . . .

LIPHITZ [*looking at* WAXMAN, *with malice*]: What an intellectual snob!

DONOVAN [*continuing*]: There might have been a bit of good-natured larking about. . . . Lippy's got a complex about Proles. . . . But . . . listen to me, Waxman. . . . We're all progressives here . . . we're all with you.

ANGEL: Waxman, I want you to listen to me. This is the easy thing to do, the obvious reaction, when you have your enemies in the corner – This –

DONOVAN: Who the hell says we're his enemies. . . ? What are you on about, Angel?

ANGEL [*ignoring him*]: When you have them in the corner . . . at your mercy . . . the easy thing to do is crush them . . . strike them down. . . . But what is the great thing to do? The mark of a man of genius. . . . A great man who can step outside his own petty prejudices and frustrations? The great thing to do is offer his hand – to help them out of their corner – to strive to conquer the corrosive hate inside him with warm healing love. . . . To consider –

[LIPHITZ *suddenly strikes* ANGEL *on the cheek.* ANGEL *shocked turns the other cheek.* LIPHITZ *strikes the other.*]

LIPHITZ [*to* WAXMAN]: That's what Angel means. . . . You see?

ANGEL [*rubbing his face*]: Waxman, you must deal charitably –

LIPHITZ: Shut up, Angel . . . will you . . . Shut up!

DONOVAN: Liphitz, if you can't do anything right, will you sit down!

LIPHITZ: She's your girl . . . not mine. . . . She's only my niece . . .

WAXMAN [*boasting*]: I could wire up that telephone just like that! In a minute! But I'm going to sit back and let you stew in your own juice. You'll see how you can do without the Proletariat.

LIPHITZ: There you see the wild animal in his true, vindictive, savage colours!

DONOVAN: Liphitz!

POSTMAN: A deadlock.

[*Pause.*]

ANGEL: It is nothing to me, Waxman. . . . But surely it would be beneficial all round if instead of Liphitz having to go out every time –

LIPHITZ: Nobody else was complaining . . .

WAXMAN: You see how you can do without the people you insult? You see? You see?

[LIPHITZ *cuts himself a slice of salami.*]

DONOVAN: Waxman, come on. . . . I'll help you . . .

WAXMAN: I'm staying here.

POSTMAN: Deadlock.

[*Door opens.* MONTY *enters. He goes up to* LIPHITZ *and shakes hands with him, then goes round the room greeting everybody formally.*]

DONOVAN: Monty, Lippy says you can wire telephones . . .

[*Door closes.*]

LIPHITZ: Monty, what have you brought me?

MONTY: I'm terribly sorry, Liphitz. I just haven't had the time to get anything. . . . I came straight from my office. You must excuse me. . . .

LIPHITZ [*sulking*]: After I had boasted about you! I said you would bring presents . . . wagonloads . . .

DONOVAN: Like an Eastern potentate he said!

MONTY [*to* DONOVAN]: I cannot wire telephones . . .

POSTMAN: Liphitz said you could.

LIPHITZ: He can do anything. . . . With money you can do anything. . . . Explain to them, Monty . . .

MONTY: I have some wine in my car, Liphitz. . . . Would you like some wine?

LIPHITZ [*delighted once more*]: Oh yes, Monty . . . I would like some wine! We were just about to start our meal. . . . That is we were waiting for you. . . . And we have no wine. . . . Monty . . . [*Makes to go out.* DONOVAN *joins him.*]

DONOVAN: I'll help you, Monty . . .

MONTY: It's not necessary . . .

DONOVAN: It's all right, I'll give you a hand . . .

[*Door opens.*]

LIPHITZ [*after them*]: Bring as many bottles as you can. . . . There's six of us. . . . [*When they are out.*] You see? He was only joking. . . . He had something all the time. . . . He's a very funny man. . . . He has a very fine sense of humour . . .

WAXMAN: That's your capitalist friend for you! He can't wire!

ANGEL: Charity, Waxman, charity. . . .

[*The knocking at the wall starts up again.*]

POSTMAN: That's the old woman knocking again, Liphitz. . . .

LIPHITZ: Help me on with my coat, will you, Angel. . . ?

ANGEL [*helping him*]: This time, it will certainly be Ruth . . . I can sense it. . . .

LIPHITZ: Well friends . . . I will give her all your love.

MONTY [*entering with* DONOVAN]: Is that Ruth now?

ANGEL: Almost certainly, Monty . . .

LIPHITZ [*going*]: The air suddenly feels colder . . . I think she's dead [*going out*].

DONOVAN: I wouldn't be surprised.

[*Door closes.*]

WAXMAN [*to* MONTY]: They've all been trying to scare me. Those operations aren't dangerous, are they?

MONTY: This is a very good man, who is attending her.

DONOVAN [*to* MONTY]: Yes? If he's as good as you make out, what the hell is he doing, carrying out abortions?

MONTY [*at loss for an explanation*]: If the worst comes to the worst . . . I have made preparations . . .

DONOVAN: Good for you, Monty! What have you done?

MONTY: I've arranged a most wonderful funeral! A Cabinet Minister couldn't have a better!

ANGEL: How many cars?

MONTY: Twenty – thirty . . . as many as you like . . . and I have given the florist a blank cheque for the flower arrangements . . .

ANGEL: As a matter of fact, I have prepared a few words for the occasion . . . just in case. . . . You have no idea how those occasions oppress me. . . . I am quite shaken up! So . . . while I have a clear head, I thought it might be as well to write it out . . .

DONOVAN: Postman'll write her epitaph . . . for the headstone . . .

POSTMAN: I've already written one or two sample verses . . .

DONOVAN: Make it clear, Postman. . . . None of your fancy, flashy obscurity . . .

MONTY: I have ordered a beautiful stone . . .

DONOVAN: What can I do?

POSTMAN: Embalm her body. . . . That's in your line, isn't it?

DONOVAN: I could too. I could make a very good job of it.
[*Pause – LIPHITZ returns.*]

WAXMAN: Was it her?

LIPHITZ: Help me off with my coat, somebody!

WAXMAN [*pulling off the coat*]: Liphitz, was it Ruth?

LIPHITZ: Not so hard! Please! You want to pull off my arms? Like a wild animal he is! I'm an old man . . . I can't be roughed up . . .

WAXMAN: Liphitz, for Christ's sake . . .

LIPHITZ [*sternly*]: Now listen to me, everybody. Ruth is dead.
[*Pause.*]

POSTMAN: Monty's making her funeral. Did you know that, Liphitz?

LIPHITZ: He can afford it!

DONOVAN: Look here, Lippy. . . . What about the order of the mourners? I think we should get that settled right away.

ANGEL: That is very important.

DONOVAN: I've seen some terrible fights over the order of mourners. I think we should get it all settled now. Once and for all. Then we won't have any trouble.

LIPHITZ [*at the table, counting the bottles of MONTY's wine*]: Only three bottles?

WAXMAN: Liphitz, can I go to the funeral?

ANGEL: My boy, perhaps it might be just as well if –

WAXMAN: Liphitz, can I go?

POSTMAN: What do you say, Liphitz? Can Waxman go to the funeral?

LIPHITZ: I'll show you exactly how it must be arranged. Donovan is quite right. A thing like that must be settled immediately. [*He indicates a chest at one wall.*] This chest is the coffin.
[*POSTMAN and DONOVAN carry the chest into the centre.*]
Put that vase on it. . . . For the flowers.

DONOVAN: Lippy, do we really need flowers? They look crappy. Victorian.

MONTY: I had ordered flowers . . .

POSTMAN: Monty gave a blank cheque to the florist.

LIPHITZ: It's a difficult question.

POSTMAN: I like flowers. But not at a funeral.

WAXMAN: Nothing's good at a funeral. . . . Flowers or anything.

LIPHITZ: Waxman, stop confusing the issue!

MONTY: I ordered flowers. . . . Ruth always loved flowers. I used to bring her some every –

LIPHITZ: Oh, let him have his flowers! We can't stand here arguing all day!

DONOVAN: That's not the point, Lippy! I still –

LIPHITZ: Stop agitating, Donovan! I said no arguments.

DONOVAN: What about the order then?

LIPHITZ: I have it in my head, the complete order. Come on, Waxman. You at the head.

WAXMAN [resisting]: No. . . . This isn't right, Liphitz. You're her uncle . . .

LIPHITZ: I said at the head. [He stands behind WAXMAN.] Now me.

POSTMAN [coming forward]: The artist next, Liphitz . . .

ANGEL: Have some sense of decency, Postman. . . . Pushing yourself forward. [He edges in front of him.]

DONOVAN: Lippy, I don't care where you put me. But if Monty's putting up the ready for the show –

LIPHITZ: Donovan next.

　　[DONOVAN hesitates.]

I'm having no arguments!

　　[DONOVAN takes up his position.]

MONTY: Liphitz, where will I stand?

LIPHITZ: Postman next.

ANGEL: She was your niece, Liphitz. . . . If you want to make an atheistic exhibition of her funeral –

LIPHITZ: Then, Angel. That's everything settled.

MONTY: Liphitz, what about me?

LIPHITZ: You? You're not coming! I'm not having a filthy capitalist at my niece's funeral! What do you think I am? You think you can buy up my soul? My religious and political principles? You think you can buy me, Liphitz, with your bloodstained pieces of silver?

POSTMAN: Amen.

DONOVAN: You're a bit hard there, Lippy. . . . Now come on –

LIPHITZ: Donovan, don't try and tell me my business! He's not coming.

WAXMAN: I think I have some say in this, Liphitz. I agree fully with the political principles you have expressed. . . . But . . . Liphitz, I think you're being unfair.

LIPHITZ: Come on. Stop arguing. Lift the coffin.

MONTY: I do feel most hurt at this heartless gesture, Liphitz.

WAXMAN [to MONTY]: I want you to come. Take my place.

LIPHITZ: He's not coming. That's final!

ANGEL: Charity, Liphitz. . . . Pity. . . . Pity, Liphitz. . . . Compassion. . . . Death knows no class barrier. . . . It is a great leveller . . .

LIPHITZ [pause, then suddenly]: Cowshit!

WAXMAN: Liphitz. I want Monty to have my place. Can he have my place?

LIPHITZ [suddenly kicking the bench away and sending the vase crashing to the ground]: He can have your place. . . . My place. . . . Anybody's place. . . . It doesn't matter . . .

DONOVAN: Steady there, Liphitz . . .

POSTMAN: Easy . . .

ANGEL: The reality of the situation is coming home to him at last, poor man.

POSTMAN: Give him some wine.

ANGEL: Liphitz, I know this is a grievous and terrible loss. . . . I will not try to minimize –

MONTY: Give him a chair. I knew there was something wrong with him.

DONOVAN: Sit down, Lippy. . . . Take it easy now . . .

LIPHITZ: It doesn't matter, I tell you. . . . Monty can have anybody's place. . . . It doesn't matter. . . . It wasn't a phone call from Ruth. . . . Not at all. . . . I thought I would mount a little joke. . . . To entertain you . . .

DONOVAN: Liphitz!

LIPHITZ: We can't have Postman's poems all the time . . . however good they may be.

DONOVAN: It wasn't Ruth?

LIPHITZ: It was some girl. . . . Looking for Fenderman. . . . She might be coming up here. . . . I told her Fenderman'll be away all week . . . I –

[WAXMAN *attacks him.*]

WAXMAN: Liphitz, you bastard! I'll murder you! I'll squeeze the last drop of life out of you!

[POSTMAN *and* DONOVAN *pull him away from* LIPHITZ.]

LIPHITZ: What an animal he is! You see him now! In his true colours! . . . I said to this girl, 'Listen, if you're doing nothing . . . I've got company now. . . . But if you come up after ten. . . .' She said she was twenty-eight. . . . That makes her about thirty-two. . . . You think that's too old?

WAXMAN: Shut up, Liphitz . . .

DONOVAN: Take it easy, Waxman. It was only a joke. . . . I saw it all the time . . .

POSTMAN: You could read it in his eyes . . .

ANGEL: We were all indulging him. . . . His tone gave him away.

WAXMAN: This is going to stop! I'm going to put an end to this once and for all!

DONOVAN: Good lad, Waxman! You're going to hook up the phone?

WAXMAN [*capitulating*]: All right . . . I'll wire it up.

DONOVAN: I'll give you a hand.

LIPHITZ: Hurry up, then, Waxman. I'm sick of taking off my coat and pulling it on again. . . . Going out in the draught. The draught is very bad for my kidneys. . . . And the old woman smells . . .

[WAXMAN *and* DONOVAN *busy themselves with preparations for the wiring job.*]

POSTMAN: All old women smell, Liphitz.

LIPHITZ: A funny smell. . . . Like lentil soup . . . going sour . . .

WAXMAN: Where's your ladder, Liphitz?

LIPHITZ: Use the chest. . . . You can put a chair on top of it . . . that'll be high enough . . .

[WAXMAN *and* DONOVAN *take the two items outside. The others go to the window to follow the operations.*]

DONOVAN [*calls from outside*]: That chest doesn't seem very strong, Lippy . . .

LIPHITZ: It's fine. . . . It'll do Waxman . . .

POSTMAN: Are you sure he can do it?

DONOVAN [*from outside*]: He's doing fine. . . . It's dead simple. . . . Just change the wires round. . . .

ANGEL: How will you feel, Liphitz, being in touch with the outside world?

LIPHITZ: Oh . . . This is exciting! I'm enjoying this! This is a great adventure! [*Dancing up and down.*] Am I not a truly adventurous man!

DONOVAN [*from outside*]: Somebody try dialling . . . will you?

LIPHITZ: Is it ready?

DONOVAN: All hooked up. . . . Go on. . . . Try and dial . . .

[LIPHITZ *goes over to the phone and dials.*]

Well?

LIPHITZ: I dialled my own number.

ANGEL: What happened?

LIPHITZ: It's engaged. Who could be speaking to me at this time of night?

DONOVAN: Stop fooling around, Lippy. . . . Dial the operator . . .

LIPHITZ: It's buzzing. . . . It's dialling away, twenty to the dozen! . . . Just like a normal natural phone! When you think about it, we should be truly thankful for telephones! It's the only healthy, normal thing about us. [*Into phone.*] Hullo . . . Hullo . . .

[WAXMAN *and* DONOVAN *return with chest and the chair. They all join him at the telephone.*]

Stop crowding round me . . . will you? Let me breathe . . . I am now in contact with the outside world . . . [*Dialling. Into phone.*] Hullo . . . Hullo . . . Liphitz here. . . . You will be delighted to hear that I am in contact with you . . . [*Hangs up.*]

POSTMAN: Who was that?

LIPHITZ [*dialling again*]: I don't know. . . . I am dialling numbers at random. [*Into phone.*] Liphitz here. . . . You will be pleased to hear that I, Liphitz, am in communication with you. . . . Please ring off now. . . . I have a number of calls to make . . .

DONOVAN: Lippy, what do you think you're doing?

LIPHITZ [*Into phone*]: Hullo . . . Hullo . . . The police? [*To the others.*] I've got the police. . . . What do you make of that?

DONOVAN: Lippy . . .

LIPHITZ [*into phone*]: Hullo? . . . Yes . . . Liphitz here. . . . What do I want? Yes . . . I'll tell you . . . I wish to report a murder.

DONOVAN: Lippy, what are you saying?

LIPHITZ: That is correct, I said a murder.

DONOVAN [*trying to pull him away*]: Lippy, get away from that phone!

LIPHITZ [*resisting him. Into phone*]: Yes. I'll hold on. . . . By all means. . . . Justice must be done. . . . That is the motive force of the universe. . . . Hullo. . . ? Hullo? Yes . . . I'll give you all the particulars. . . . I am Liphitz . . . Twenty-three Burntree Gardens. . . . I want to report a murder. . . . A young girl. . . . Twenty-two. Ruth Liphitz. . . . My niece. . . . Good. . . . Excellent. . . . I want to see justice done. . . . As I was remarking to the other officer on the phone, that is the mainspring of our universe. . . . Yes? You ask who committed the crime? That is a difficult question. . . . Complicated. . . . Involved. . . . I, Liphitz, certainly was one of the murderers. . . . Postman, Donovan, Angel, Monty, Waxman . . . Waxman . . . above all. . . . Yes . . . Waxman stands out among us.

WAXMAN [*with sudden insight*]: Yes . . . He's right. . . . Liphitz is right. . . . I'm the worst. . . . Me above all . . .

LIPHITZ [*putting the phone down*]: They're coming right away. What a useful thing a telephone is!

MONTY: Liphitz, thank you . . . thank you . . . thank you, Liphitz . . .

LIPHITZ: It's all right. It's a pleasure, Monty. You see, when I got on to the police . . . I knew that something was on my mind . . .

ANGEL [*about to deliver a sermon*]: When he lifted up that telephone and said: 'Hullo . . . Police? This is –'

DONOVAN: Yes! We all know what he said!

ANGEL: The room was filled with light!

POSTMAN: That's exactly how I felt. . . . It was a shaft of pure light . . . in a black room . . .

LIPHITZ: Listen, everybody! Keep quiet! Waxman is thinking! Can you hear him? Can you hear the drops of pure thought dripping from his cerebellum?

WAXMAN: I am guilty, Liphitz. . . . You're right.

ANGEL: We are all guilty.

DONOVAN: Don't be so greedy, Waxman! Don't hog all the guilt for yourself!

LIPHITZ: That's Waxman all along!

WAXMAN: I am the guiltiest.

ANGEL: What do you think of that, Liphitz?

WAXMAN: Liphitz, I was supposed to love her . . .

POSTMAN: What do you think, Liphitz?

DONOVAN: He's certainly the leading criminal. Didn't even pay her!

MONTY: Waxman struck the final blow.

LIPHITZ: Wasn't that a good idea? A wonderful idea? Bringing all that guilt right out – naked, into the open! What couldn't a lovely, intelligent, alive girl like Ruth have achieved – if we would have allowed her to come to fruit. . . ? She could have inherited the earth. . . . I ask you. . . . Couldn't she have inherited the earth?

ANGEL [*in pain*]: Liphitz, don't! Please. . . . Don't!

LIPHITZ: Now we have uncovered this guilt. . . . What is the next step? Waxman, what would you say is the next step? Now your brain is actually pulsating. . . . dripping thoughts. . . . What is to be done now?

ANGEL: Our next move.

LIPHITZ: You shut up, Angel! Let Waxman speak.

WAXMAN [*thinking*]: I should be punished. . . . Badly punished. . . . There is no punishment good enough for me!

LIPHITZ: You are right, Waxman. You are perfectly right!

WAXMAN [*shouting*]: I should be hanged!
[*They all stare at him.*]
I'm telling you. . . . I should be hanged!

LIPHITZ: Listen to me, Waxman. Would you really like to be hanged, Waxman?

WAXMAN: It would only be justice . . .

LIPHITZ: All right then, Waxman. We'll hang you.

WAXMAN: I don't want to put anybody to any trouble.

LIPHITZ: That's perfectly all right, Waxman. We'll hang you.

DONOVAN: Where are you going to hang him, Lippy? That's the point.

LIPHITZ: I'm not having you hung up here and messing up all the room, if that's what you think, Waxman!

WAXMAN: I'm not dictating where, Liphitz. Anywhere will do me.

POSTMAN: What about the garden?

ANGEL: The garden would be ideal! You have that lovely pear tree. . . . That would be perfect . . .

LIPHITZ: The garden's out! I don't want all the neighbours to know my business. . . . In any case, it's too cold . . .

DONOVAN: Pity we haven't a gun.

WAXMAN: A gun would be no use. That wouldn't be justice.

DONOVAN: Yes. True enough. Too quick.

POSTMAN: Pht! And he's finished.

ANGEL: There's no ceremony with a gun. No sense of occasion . . .

DONOVAN: I don't know. What about a military execution. . . ?

ANGEL: Yes. . . . But there you have rifles . . . and a firing squad . . .

MONTY: What about the lavatory? Haven't you some kind of a pulley up there?

LIPHITZ: Perfect! That would be perfect! How do you feel about being hung in the lavatory, Waxman?

WAXMAN: I don't mind where you do it! Only get on with it! If you mess about too long, the police'll be here and –

LIPHITZ: Listen, Waxman, don't rush me. You hear me? I will not be rushed.

DONOVAN: What about some rope?

ANGEL [going out]: Excuse me, a minute, please . . .

LIPHITZ: Where do you think you're going?

ANGEL: Before you . . . do it . . . I'd like to relieve myself.

LIPHITZ: You're a fastidious type, Angel, aren't you. . . . Why can't you wait?

ANGEL: If you don't mind, Liphitz . . . [Going out.]

LIPHITZ: Anybody else feel like him?

WAXMAN: I think I'll go up.

LIPHITZ: Certainly, Waxman, a pleasure!

POSTMAN: Waxman, would you have any last request?

DONOVAN: Yes. That's important. How about it, Waxman?

WAXMAN [thinking]: I don't know.

LIPHITZ: Let him get upstairs and attend to his business, will you?

WAXMAN: I'll think about it . . . [Going out.]

DONOVAN: Where's the rope, Liphitz?

LIPHITZ: It's not a thing I keep lying about the house . . .

DONOVAN: He's a hefty man, Liphitz.

LIPHITZ [producing some electric cable from a drawer]: Here, what do you think of this, Donovan?

DONOVAN [running his hand over it, stretching it]: Pretty strong . . . and smooth. . . . Yes. . . . Make a good noose this. . . . Fine . . .

ANGEL [entering]: I would have preferred a rope.

LIPHITZ: We haven't got a rope. It'll have to be this cable.

ANGEL: A rope would be more in keeping with the ceremony.

LIPHITZ [angrily]: I said we haven't got a rope!

ANGEL: I will say a few appropriate words . . .

LIPHITZ: You'll shut up, that's what you'll do! I don't want any of your moanings and incantations and black magic here! I want a

dignified, twentieth-century execution. This is a classic situation . . .
Six guilty men executing a seventh.

DONOVAN: Who's going to be hangman?

LIPHITZ: You're the scientist.

DONOVAN: I don't mind. I just thought . . . maybe somebody else
fancied the job. . . . I've got a good idea what's needed . . .

ANGEL: I envy Waxman! If I could only be relieved of my guilt so
quickly!

LIPHITZ: We're not going to hang you as well, if that's what you
think! That's final!

DONOVAN: That would make a mockery of the whole thing!

LIPHITZ: Waxman was the first to speak in any case . . .

DONOVAN: I'm certainly not hanging any more . . .

LIPHITZ: As for the rest of us, the police are on their way. They will
attend to us . . .

ANGEL: It's the agony of waiting, Liphitz. . . . The trial – the interro-
gation . . . all the formalities . . .

LIPHITZ: I don't care what agony you're in, Angel. That's my final
word on it!

[WAXMAN enters.]

ANGEL: You're a lucky man, Waxman.

DONOVAN: Are you ready, Waxman?

WAXMAN: I am.

LIPHITZ: Take some wine, before you go up, Waxman. [He pours out
two glasses.] Some cornflakes?

WAXMAN: Just a few.

[LIPHITZ heaps cornflakes in a plate. WAXMAN eats with his wine.]

LIPHITZ: Take an apple. . . . You can eat it while we're going up,
Waxman. So? What is everybody waiting for? What's the matter
with you, Monty?

MONTY: If you don't mind, Liphitz. . . . I'd rather wait here. I will
accept equal responsibility with you all for Waxman. But . . .

LIPHITZ: Monty, if you are looking at this matter on the grounds of
Capital Punishment, let me explain this immediately. This is not
Capital Punishment. This is Capital Atonement.

MONTY: I'd rather wait here, Liphitz.

LIPHITZ: Waxman will be disappointed.

WAXMAN: I'm not. If he wants to wait here . . . I don't mind.

LIPHITZ: We're all disappointed . . .

MONTY: I'm sorry, Liphitz.

LIPHITZ: That's you all over, Monty! You'd think it's the least you could do! [*Corking the winebottle.*] We'll drink afterwards.

[*They all follow* LIPHITZ *out.* MONTY *sinks into a chair. He covers his face with his hands. Various noises, shuffling feet, banging. The pulley can be heard being pulled down. A pause, then more shuffling. The pulley is then slowly heaved up.*]

VOICE [*off*]: That's the stuff! Very fine!

ANGEL [*off*]: The Lord giveth and the Lord taketh away. Blessed be the name of the Lord for ever and ever!

[MONTY *groans. Then he stands up.* LIPHITZ *returns, followed by the others. Light-hearted laughter.*]

MONTY: Did it go well?

LIPHITZ: The pulley worked excellently, Monty.

POSTMAN: Donovan did a good job, Monty.

DONOVAN: I had a good idea how it was to be done.

ANGEL: A most dignified, moving ceremony.

POSTMAN: He went like a hero, mind you! Didn't he?

DONOVAN: Out like a light, Monty! First-class job, though I said it myself!

LIPHITZ: You know your science, Donovan! Monty, you should have been there. Angel's mouth was watering. Did you notice Angel's mouth?

MONTY: Some wine?

LIPHITZ: You can give them a glass each. But not too full.

[MONTY *begins to pour the wine.*]

[*To* ANGEL.] Of course you had to come out with your incantations!

ANGEL: Just a short prayer, Liphitz.

POSTMAN: I thought it fitted in very well. Sort of finished off the ceremony.

DONOVAN: Yes, Lippy . . . I'm not a religious type myself. But it did impart some design to the ceremony.

LIPHITZ: Imparted some design! Imparted some wetness! Some black magic . . . knocked it all off balance . . .

ANGEL: Everyone is entitled to his own opinion. This is a democracy, after all. . . . Tolerance, mutual respect, those are –

LIPHITZ [*suddenly dancing up and down*]: I've never felt better in my life! I could dance! [*Sings.*]

> Happy days are here again,
> All the skies are blue and clear again,
> Let us sing a song of cheer again,
> Happy days are here again!

All together now . . .

> Happy days are here again,
> All the skies are blue and clear again,
> Let us sing a song of cheer again,
> Happy days are here again!

POSTMAN: I feel so free! Suddenly! Lighter . . . like a feather . . . a cloud . . .

ANGEL: So do I, Postman. . . . I feel lighter. . . . Almost happy . . .

DONOVAN: Yes . . . I've got a bit of the Easter rabbit in me myself now!

MONTY: It happened to me a few minutes ago. Just before you came down.

LIPHITZ: Of course you all feel free.

> [*Pause.*]

DONOVAN: What about you, Lippy?

LIPHITZ: It was obvious what was going to happen. The minute Waxman went, the weight would be lifted.

POSTMAN: That's exactly what happened. Liphitz, you're right!

LIPHITZ: Of course I'm right.

DONOVAN: Yes. I let the rope go. Waxman swung . . . and went out . . .

ANGEL: And we were born again! Well we were, weren't we, Liphitz. . . ?

MONTY: It happened to me, even out of the room. . . . Down here. . . . I had a sudden feeling of freedom. . . . As if I had thrown off all my worries . . . all my responsibilities and was about to go on a long holiday . . .

LIPHITZ: What do you expect? That was the idea. . . . We heaped all our guilt on top of Waxman . . . piled it up . . . up to his neck . . . till his back was breaking with it. . . . And he carried it all away with him.

ANGEL: And the goat shall bear upon all their iniquities, unto a land not inhabited . . .

LIPHITZ: Look here, Angel! We've had enough of that!

> [*Pause.*]

DONOVAN: What should we do now, Lippy?

LIPHITZ: Got to do something with our new-found freedom. Should we go out and look for women? I would like to do this. Speaking as a sex-obsessed lecher, Angel, would you advise this?

ANGEL: I would like to go for a long walk in the country. . . . Ten miles.

LIPHITZ: In this weather!

DONOVAN: Cool his blood! . . . Personally, I fancy a good booze-up. . . . All right . . .

LIPHITZ: Are you writing a poem, Postman?

POSTMAN: Just an idea, Liphitz. . . . Sketching it out . . .

MONTY: I would like to go into the town and spend money.

LIPHITZ: Buy a new car, Monty?

MONTY: Something nice. . . . I never really enjoyed anything before. I had this load on me all the time. . . . Ever since that first time with Ruth . . .

DONOVAN: Oh, don't be so sorry for yourself, Monty! We were all exactly the same!

POSTMAN [*rising*]: I can't get it down on paper. . . . In the correct design. . . . I want to say, now we can go out and enjoy life. . . . Free. . . . The shadow is no longer there, to mar our pleasure.

MONTY: Yes . . . I think I'll go into town.

DONOVAN: You can give me a run to the Barley Mill.

ANGEL: And me to the Bus Station.

[*They all make to get ready . . . But* LIPHITZ *stops them.*]

LIPHITZ: Listen! You're all mad! Where do you think you're going? You can't leave this house. The police will be here in a minute. What do you think? You can run away from the police?

[*They stand, all their gaiety gone, dejected. Pause.*]

Yes. . . . It's a pity we phoned the police, after all . . .

POSTMAN: Now they'll come and spoil everything!

DONOVAN [*angrily*]: You were a bit quick with that phone, Liphitz.

LIPHITZ: Yes. I was very quick, wasn't I? Mind you, I'm always like that . . . with that tendency to quickness . . .

POSTMAN: Didn't even stop to think!

ANGEL: Who asked you to phone the police, anyway?

LIPHITZ: That's right! Go on! Make a scapegoat out of me! That's why I was born. To be a scapegoat. I, Liphitz! The eternal scapegoat. But you can't do a thing about it now. They've been sent for.

And they will be coming. And they will carry us off. Interrogate us. Try us. And execute us. . . . But all in a businesslike, professional manner . . . I can assure you.

ANGEL: Couldn't we say it was a mistake about Ruth. . . . After all, there still –

LIPHITZ [*raging*]: Civilized people. . . . Progressive people. . . . Supposedly intelligent. . . . Making a scapegoat out of an old man!

POSTMAN: They'll hang us for hanging Waxman.

LIPHITZ: But I refuse to be thrown back into my historical role! You hear me? This time I am not going to be –

DONOVAN: Lippy, you're up the pole!

ANGEL: When you think about it, deeply . . . Waxman was really the murderer. We were only carrying out the justice of the Lord.

MONTY: Angel's perfectly right. She was happy and gay and light-hearted before she met Waxman.

POSTMAN: It was like a black cloud over a shining brook.

DONOVAN: Look. It's obvious. The thing to do is hide Waxman.

LIPHITZ [*pouring himself out some more wine*]: You and your chameleon ideas! Restless . . . a pest . . . always on the move . . . a neurotic!

DONOVAN: What do you say? When the police come, we can tell them that Waxman was the murderer . . . and he's run away . . .

LIPHITZ: I wish you would stop confusing my designs, Donovan! You hear me! I like to make a plan –

DONOVAN: Liphitz, where can we hide Waxman?

MONTY: Just till the police go away. After that I'll take him away in my car. I can dispose of him.

LIPHITZ [*to* MONTY]: That's the least you could do! And please don't say it in that patronizing, generous manner. . . . As if you're doing us all a great favour.

DONOVAN: Liphitz, shut up!

LIPHITZ: It's easy for him to help. He has a car. . . . Nobody else has a car. . . .

MONTY: Liphitz, I accept all my responsibilities.

LIPHITZ: That's fine then. Accept all your responsibilities and shut up! Shut up, Monty!

DONOVAN: Liphitz, where can we put Waxman?

POSTMAN: Why can't we leave him where he is?

LIPHITZ: And let us suppose, Postman, one of the police has a weak bladder. . . . This is highly possible. . . . They live under great stresses. . . . Postman, you have the imagination of a clothes-peg manufacturer!

DONOVAN: Lippy! We haven't much time!

LIPHITZ: Hide him in the cupboard there. Then we won't have so far to carry him out to the car, when the police are finished.

MONTY: Isn't that rather dangerous! The police will be in this room.

LIPHITZ: We'll wrap him up in an old sheet and he'll be fine . . .

DONOVAN: Can you lock that cupboard, Lippy?

LIPHITZ: Donovan, will you stop wasting time?

DONOVAN: All right, Lippy. . . . All right. . . . Who's going to give us a hand. . . ?

   [*They all follow* DONOVAN *out, except* MONTY. *Pause. They approach carrying* WAXMAN, *wrapped up in an old sheet. They place him in the cupboard.*]

LIPHITZ: Hold the door. Right, push him in. Shut the door now.

ANGEL: Isn't it a bit risky, Liphitz?

LIPHITZ: I will meet the police all smiles. With an open manner. . . . I will say to them – what do you think I should say to them, Postman – speaking as a literary expert?

DONOVAN: That's right, Postman. . . . You concoct the story.

POSTMAN: Gentlemen,
                 The Telephone
                 Has some strange power
                 Over my wits . . .
                 Taking it up
                 This afternoon
                 The rasping
                 The buzzing
                 Created confusion
                 In my mind.

DONOVAN: All right.

LIPHITZ: This is very true. This is exactly how I felt . . .

POSTMAN [*continuing*]:
                 So that
                 On hearing your request
                 For information –
                 For facts,
                 My confusion
                 My anxiety to please,

My desire to be loved,
To be your man,
Caused me
To fabricate,
To spin
This fantasy
Which drew you,
Gentlemen,
To my house.

DONOVAN: Brilliant!

LIPHITZ: And following on this explanation, I shall, of course, apologize for taking up their time. . .

ANGEL: What about Waxman?

LIPHITZ: Yes. . . . What about that, Postman. . . ?

POSTMAN: I was coming to that, Liphitz.
But fantasies,
And fairy tales,
Like spiders' webs,
Are built from solid stuff,
Thus my fantasy
The result
Of rape
Of corruption
Of my niece,
One Ruth,
Sixteen,
As sweet,
As Juliet!

LIPHITZ: Not strictly true. . . . But it gives me the ring of greatness . . .

DONOVAN: Catches their sympathy too . . .

POSTMAN: But Waxman,
A flesh man –

LIPHITZ: I've got the gist.

POSTMAN: I was nearly finished, Liphitz.
But Waxman –

LIPHITZ: That's enough, Postman! Those literary maniacs!

DONOVAN: It's not bad, for impromptu . . .

LIPHITZ: That's all he's good for, improvisation. Let's have some cornflakes while we're waiting . . . and apples . . . [*He doles them out of the bag.*] None left for you, Angel.

ANGEL: You didn't need to give Waxman an apple.

LIPHITZ: He enjoyed that apple. He really did. Did you see him?

ANGEL: Considering there wasn't enough to go round . . .

LIPHITZ: Whose fault was that, Angel?

[*They all begin to eat.* LIPHITZ *watches them.* DONOVAN *tries to throw off the mood.*]

DONOVAN [*singing, but flatly, with no spirit*]:

Happy days are here again,
All the skies . . . [*He breaks off.*]

LIPHITZ [*standing*]: There you are! You see! You didn't listen to me. I told you. When I make a plan, leave it alone. Stop messing about with it . . .

DONOVAN: Lippy, what are you moaning about now?

LIPHITZ: It's back, isn't it? Heavier than ever!

DONOVAN: What's back?

ANGEL: Liphitz means the guilt.

MONTY: I thought you couldn't stay happy as that for long.

POSTMAN: It was such a beautiful feeling! I was on a high ridge of mountains. The snow was turning pink with the setting sun. Mountain hares jumped about me as I walked. . . . Like animated lumps of snow.

DONOVAN: It's no use. Lippy's right. It was hiding Waxman. . . . As soon as we stuck him in that cupboard. . . . It was all finished.

MONTY: Liphitz, what can we do? Liphitz, what can we do?

LIPHITZ: I told you what to do!

DONOVAN: We'll have to bring Waxman out into the open.

MONTY: And when the police come, admit we hung Waxman.

LIPHITZ [*at the window*]: The police are coming now. . . . Two cars of them!

MONTY: Liphitz, you'll have to tell the police.

[*The police knock.* LIPHITZ *opens the door. The* DETECTIVE *enters.*]

DETECTIVE: You are Liphitz?

LIPHITZ: You've been a long time. But don't apologize.

DONOVAN: Give us time to straighten out our affairs . . .

LIPHITZ: This is Donovan . . .

DETECTIVE: Are all those men involved?

LIPHITZ: Oh, yes. . . . Most certainly . . .

DETECTIVE: Where is the girl?

LIPHITZ: The girl! [*To the others.*] The Detective has raised a most important question.

DETECTIVE: There is some doubt as to the location of the girl's body?

LIPHITZ: Exactly, sir. That is very well put. A most excellent explanation. [*To the others.*] Isn't it, gentlemen? [*To the* DETECTIVE *again.*] Yes, sir . . .

DETECTIVE: Your accomplices. Have they information, as to the body's location?

LIPHITZ: Listen, sir. . . . I struck the first blow.

DONOVAN: You, Liphitz!

LIPHITZ: I'm telling you. I struck the first blow. . . . [*To* DETECTIVE.] Some wine, sir? I'm about to have a glass. [*He pours out two glasses, handing one to the* DETECTIVE.]

DETECTIVE: Thank you.
    [*They both drink.*]

LIPHITZ: I had run short of cash. Ruth was just a year out of school. Working in a chemist shop . . .

DONOVAN: About sixteen?

LIPHITZ: Yes . . . sixteen. . . . That was exactly her age . . . [*To* DETECTIVE.] She wasn't bad at sixteen. . . . But nothing like as ravishing as she was later. . . . I'm not one of those people that rave about the attractiveness of teenagers. . . . I prefer them a shade or so older. . . . But at the time I was short of cash. . . . Hadn't had a girl in weeks . . .

DETECTIVE: I can sympathize.

LIPHITZ: My appetites aren't all that great. . . . More or less normal. . . . But you understand . . . they exist . . .

DETECTIVE: Of course.

LIPHITZ: One summer's night. . . Wednesday, if you wish to make a note. Her bedroom was next to mine. [*He throws his empty wineglass on the floor.*] An explosive situation . . . you see . . . [*He lifts his foot and brings it crashing down on the glass.*] Ignited by a spark of lust!
    [*Pause.*]
    Then there was Waxman . . .

DETECTIVE: Yes . . . I have Waxman on the list . . .

LIPHITZ: A foul, obscene, mentally retarded, puritanical hypocrite! An Oliver Cromwell, if you know what I mean. Speaking as an experienced enforcer of the law, what punishment would you recommend for a man like that?

DETECTIVE: I know the type.

LIPHITZ: We hung Waxman. Just a short time ago . . .

[*The telephone rings.*]

[*Into phone.*] Hullo? Hullo? [*To the others.*] It's Ruth. . . . Hullo dear. . . . Yes . . . I'm fine. . . . We've had an exciting time. . . . What with one thing and another. . . . All your friends are here. . . . Postman . . . Donovan . . . Everybody . . . I had a party for them. . . . We had –

DONOVAN: Ask her how she is.

LIPHITZ: What you think, Ruth? Monty. . . . He didn't bring a thing. Waxman brought raisins . . .

POSTMAN: Ask her how the operation went?

DONOVAN: Has she had it?

LIPHITZ [*turning from the phone*]: Listen, shut up, will you. I can't do two things at once. . . . I either speak to Ruth or listen to you. Which do you want?

MONTY [*pleading*]: Liphitz, please, we want to know what happened.

LIPHITZ [*into phone*]: They want to know how the 'you know what' went? . . . You didn't have it. . . . Listen, Ruth darling. . . . Please yourself . . .

MONTY: She didn't have it! After everything was arranged!

LIPHITZ [*into phone*]: I'm very pleased to hear it dear. . . . Listen, I know. . . . Nobody could love Waxman. . . . I don't know what you should do. . . . Listen, we had an interesting afternoon. . . . Ruth. . . . I don't know. . . . I suppose a baby is something to love. . . . No doubt. . . . But we had a regular party. . . . You don't love Waxman. . . . Or the others? . . . No. . . . I can understand. . . . Yes. . . . Hullo. . . . Hullo . . . Operator. . . . Hullo. . . . [*To the others.*] She's run out of change . . .

MONTY: Liphitz, why didn't Ruth?

DETECTIVE: That was the girl?

LIPHITZ: Ruth, my niece.

DETECTIVE: Speaking from where?

LIPHITZ: London. Listen, we're all friends here . . . she'd gone to procure an abortion.

ANGEL [*quickly*]: Owing to a heart condition.

DONOVAN: She had a doctor's certificate.

189

DETECTIVE: The girl is alive.

[*They all suddenly realize the fact.*]

MONTY: Ruth's alive. . . . Ruth's alive!

POSTMAN: And most of her life is still in front of her.

MONTY: She's alive.

ANGEL: We may have struck a severe blow at a crucial stage in her life. . . . But time is a great healer . . .

MONTY: Ruth's alive!

DETECTIVE: Certainly, she is alive. . . . Most certainly.

LIPHITZ: Play with words! She's alive! What's alive? What does that mean, alive? A pig's alive. . . . A horse is alive . . .

POSTMAN [*to* DETECTIVE]: Liphitz hypnotized us.

DONOVAN: With his shitty philosophy.

ANGEL: He turned the truth on its head.

MONTY: We were all under severe emotional stress. . . . Liphitz threw a fog over us, Inspector.

ANGEL: You see, Inspector, the telephone call of Liphitz was really the result of a simple misunderstanding. . . . What actually happened –

[*While they are speaking,* LIPHITZ *goes to the cupboard. He pulls open the door and* WAXMAN's *body falls out on to the floor.* ANGEL *breaks off. They all stare at the corpse.* DONOVAN *is the first to take the initiative.*]

DONOVAN: Liphitz, who's that?

MONTY: Did you know about that, Liphitz?

ANGEL: It seems to be a dead man, Liphitz. In your cupboard.

POSTMAN: How did he get there, Liphitz?

LIPHITZ [*to* DETECTIVE]: This is Waxman.

DETECTIVE [*consulting notebook*]: Waxman?

LIPHITZ: You have him on your list. . . . We hung him. In the lavatory.

DONOVAN: What you on about, Lippy?

ANGEL: What are you trying to say, Liphitz? The poor man's mind is wandering.

POSTMAN: Take a grip of yourself, Liphitz. Try to be coherent.

MONTY [*to* DETECTIVE]: He's obviously hysterical, Inspector.

DETECTIVE: Who is this Waxman?

MONTY: Waxman? Waxman?

DONOVAN: Never heard of him.

ANGEL: Waxman. Can't say the name rings a bell.

POSTMAN: Friend of yours, is he, Liphitz?

LIPHITZ [*watching them. With scorn at the poverty of their invention*]:
Listen to them! Go try to lift him, Inspector. . . . Like a mountain,
he is! I could lift a dead weight like that. . . . On my own?

DONOVAN: The old man's wandering, Inspector . . .

ANGEL: Shouldn't he be given a sedative, Inspector?

LIPHITZ: Angel. . . . Listen. . . . Listen to me. Look at him, Angel.
Look at Waxman, Angel. . . . Remember. . . . Remember, Angel. . . .
How your mouth watered – as the life ran from his body.

ANGEL [*crying out*]: Don't, Liphitz. . . . Don't!

LIPHITZ: And you, Postman. When Waxman was swinging.
Remember. . . . How you scribbled like a madman to get down
every sensation. . . . It's in your notebook, Postman. You have it all
down. [*Turning to* MONTY.] Monty. . . . You don't remember what
happened . . . when we came down. . . . How you were standing. . . .
Like in Paradise . . .

MONTY: Yes, Liphitz. . . . Like in Paradise.

LIPHITZ: And you, Mr Bachelor of Science, Donovan. . . . [*Reaching
into his pocket and producing the noose.*] Don't you want to show the
Inspector your little souvenir . . . your marvel of ingenuity? Take a
look, Inspector. . . . Just a length of flex . . . a piece of cable. [*Turning
to his friends.*] So . . . come, gentlemen. Don't keep the inspector
waiting . . .

   [*They begin to line up.*]
You think ours are the only executions in this world?

END